FOUNDATION 2/ HIGHER 1

MASTERING MATHEMATICS

FOR OCR GCSE

Practice • Reinforcement • Progress

Assessment Consultant and Editor: **Keith Pledger**

Keith Pledger, Gareth Cole and Joe Petran

Series Editor: Roger Porkess

HODDER EDUCATION
AN HACHETTE UK COMPANY

Although every effort has been made to ensure that website addresses are correct at time of going to press, Hodder Education cannot be held responsible for the content of any website mentioned. It is sometimes possible to find a relocated web page by typing in the address of the home page for a website in the URL window of your browser.

Orders: please contact Bookpoint Ltd, 130 Milton Park, Abingdon, Oxon OX14 4SB.
Telephone: (44) 01235 827720. Fax: (44) 01235 400454. Lines are open 9.00–17.00, Monday to Saturday, with a 24-hour message answering service. Visit our website at www.hoddereducation.co.uk

© Keith Pledger, Gareth Cole, Joe Petran 2016

First published in 2016 by

Hodder Education

An Hachette UK Company,

50 Victoria Embankment

London EC4Y 0DZ

Impression number   5   4   3   2   1

Year   2019   2018   2017   2016

All rights reserved. Apart from any use permitted under UK copyright law, no part of this publication may be reproduced or transmitted in any form or by any means, electronic or mechanical, including photocopying and recording, or held within any information storage and retrieval system, without permission in writing from the publisher or under licence from the Copyright Licensing Agency Limited.

Further details of such licences (for reprographic reproduction) may be obtained from the Copyright Licensing Agency Limited, Saffron House, 6–10 Kirby Street, London EC1N 8TS.

Cover photo © Spectral-Design – Fotolia

Illustrations by Integra

Typeset in India by Integra Software Services Pvt. Ltd., Pondicherry

Printed in Great Britain by CPI Group (UK) Ltd, Croydon CR0 4YY

A catalogue record for this title is available from the British Library

ISBN 978 1471 874536

Contents

How to get the most from this book — vii

NUMBER

Strand 2 Using our number system
Unit 7 Calculating with standard form — 1

Strand 3 Accuracy
Unit 7 Limits of accuracy — 4

Strand 5 Percentages
Unit 6 Reverse percentages — 7
Unit 7 Repeated percentage increase/decrease — 9

Strand 6 Ratio and proportion
Unit 4 The constant of proportionality — 12
Unit 5 Working with inversely proportional quantities — 15

Strand 7 Number properties
Unit 4 Index notation — 18
Unit 5 Prime factorisation — 20
Unit 6 Rules of indices — 23

ALGEBRA

Strand 1 Starting algebra
Unit 7 Working with more complex equations — 26
Unit 8 Solving equations with brackets — 28
Unit 9 Simplifying harder expressions — 30
Unit 10 Using complex formulae — 32
Unit 11 Identities — 34

Strand 2 Sequences

Unit 5 Quadratic sequences	36
Unit 6 Geometric progressions	38

Strand 3 Functions and graphs

Unit 5 Finding equations of straight lines	40
Unit 6 Quadratic functions	43
Unit 7 Polynomial and reciprocal functions	46

Strand 4 Algebraic methods

Unit 2 Linear inequalities	48
Unit 3 Solving pairs of equations by substitution	50
Unit 4 Solving simultaneous equations by elimination	52
Unit 5 Using graphs to solve simultaneous equations	54

Strand 5 Working with quadratics

Unit 1 Factorising quadratics	56
Unit 2 Solving equations by factorising	58

GEOMETRY AND MEASURES

Strand 1 Units and scales

Unit 11 Working with compound units	60

Strand 2 Properties of shapes

Unit 9 Congruent triangles and proof	63
Unit 10 Proof using similar and congruent triangles	66

Strand 3 Measuring shapes

Unit 5 Pythagoras' theorem	69
Unit 6 Arcs and sectors	71

Strand 4 Construction

Unit 3 Constructions with a pair of compasses	74
Unit 4 Loci	77

Strand 5 Transformations

Unit 7 Similarity	80
Unit 8 Trigonometry	83
Unit 9 Trigonometry for special angles	86
Unit 10 Finding centres of rotation	88

Strand 6 Three-dimensional shapes

Unit 7 Constructing plans and elevations	91
Unit 8 Surface area and volume of 3D shapes	93

Strand 7 Vectors

Unit 1 Vectors	96

STATISTICS AND PROBABILITY

Strand 2 Draw and interpret statistical diagrams

Unit 5 Displaying grouped data	98
Unit 6 Scatter diagrams	102
Unit 7 Using lines of best fit	107

Strand 4 Probability

Unit 4 Estimating probability	111
Unit 5 The multiplication rule	114
Unit 6 The addition rule	117

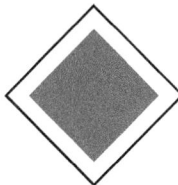

How to get the most from this book

Introduction

This book is part of the Mastering Mathematics for OCR GCSE series and supports the textbook by providing lots of extra practice questions for the Foundation 2, Higher 1 tier.

This Practice Book is structured to match the Foundation 2/Higher 1 Student's Book and is likewise organised by key areas of the specification: Number, Algebra, Geometry & Measures and Statistics & Probability. Every chapter in this book accompanies its corresponding chapter from the textbook, with matching titles for ease of use.

Please note: the 'Moving On' units in the Student's Book cover prior knowledge only, so do not have accompanying chapters in this Practice Book. For this reason, although the running order of the Practice Book follows the Student's Book, you may notice that some Strand/Unit numbers appear to be missing, or do not start at '1'.

Progression through each chapter

Chapters include a range of questions that increase in difficulty as you progress through the exercise. There are three levels of difficulty across the Student's Books and Practice Books in this series. These are denoted by shaded spots on the right hand side of each page. Levels broadly reflect GCSE Maths grades as follows:

Low difficulty	GCSE Maths grades 1–3	●○○
Medium difficulty	GCSE Maths grades 4–6	●●○
High difficulty	GCSE Maths grades 7–9	●●●

You might wish to start at the beginning of each chapter and work through so you can see how you are progressing.

Question types

There is also a range of question types included in each chapter, which are denoted by codes to the left hand side of the question or sub-question where they appear. These are examples of the types of question that you will need to practice in readiness for the GCSE Maths exam.

PS Practising skills

These questions are all about building and mastering the essential techniques that you need to succeed.

How to get the most from this book

DF Developing fluency

These give you practice of using your skills for a variety of purposes and contexts, building your confidence to tackle any type of question.

PB Problem solving

These give practice of using your problem solving skills in order to tackle more demanding problems in the real world, in other subjects and within Maths itself.

Next to any question, including the above question types, you may also see the below code. This means that it is an exam-style question.

ES Exam style

This question reflects the language, style and wording of a question that you might see in your GCSE Maths exam.

Answers

There are answers to every question within the book on our website.

Please visit: www.hoddereducation.co.uk/MasteringmathsforOCRGCSE

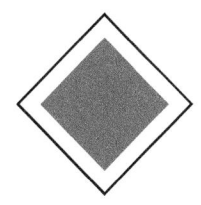

Number Strand 2 Using our number system Unit 7 Calculating with standard form

PS PRACTISING SKILLS **DF** DEVELOPING FLUENCY **PB** PROBLEM SOLVING **ES** EXAM-STYLE

PS 1 Copy and complete each of the following. Replace each letter with the missing number.
   a $5.85 \times 10^5 + 2.35 = a \times 10^5$
   b $1.97 \times 10^{-3} + 2.8 \times 10^{-3} = b \times 10^{-3}$
   c $7.09 \times 10^7 - 6.3 \times 10^7 = c \times 10^6$
   d $9.4 \times 10^{-5} + 9.4 \times 10^{-5} = d \times 10^{-4}$

PS 2 Work out the value of the following, giving your answers in standard form.
   a $3.25 \times 10^4 + 2.75 \times 10^4$
   b $6.21 \times 10^{-8} - 4.6 \times 10^{-8}$
   c $8.9 \times 10^3 + 2.95 \times 10^3$
   d $6.35 \times 10^{-6} + 5.04 \times 10^{-6}$
   e $8.9 \times 10^5 - 8.6 \times 10^5$
   f $3.19 \times 10^{-2} - 3.14 \times 10^{-2}$

PS 3 Work out the following, giving your answers in standard form.
   a $100 \times 1.8 \times 10^6$
   b $1000 \times 9.3 \times 10^7$
   c $10000 \times 2.7 \times 10^{-2}$
   d $5.3 \times 10^7 \div 1000$
   e $1.03 \times 10^3 \div 10000$
   f $1.2 \times 10^{-4} \div 100$

PS 4 Without using a calculator, work out the value of the following. Give your answers in standard form.
   a $3.4 \times 10^5 \times 1.9 \times 10^3$
   b $2.8 \times 10^{-4} \times 3.6 \times 10^6$
   c $7.2 \times 10^{-3} \times 2.5 \times 10^{-2}$
   d $4.8 \times 10^9 \div 5 \times 10^4$
   e $3.2 \times 10^4 \div 8 \times 10^{-5}$
   f $9 \times 10^{-1} \div 1.5 \times 10^{-3}$

DF 5 Given that $x = 3.5 \times 10^5$, $y = 1.8 \times 10^2$ and $z = 2 \times 10^{-3}$, work out the value of the following. Give your answers in standard form.
   a xy
   b $\frac{x}{z}$
   c x^2
   d z^3
   e xyz
   f x^{-3}

1

Number Strand 2 Using our number system Unit 7 Calculating with standard form

6 Use the information in the table to answer the following. Give your answers in standard form.

| 1 kilowatt = 10^3 watts |
| 1 megawatt = 10^6 watts |
| 1 gigawatt = 10^9 watts |
| 1 terawatt = 10^{12} watts |

  a Change 230 gigawatts to watts.
  b Change 0.25 gigawatts to kilowatts.
  c Change 125 kilowatts to megawatts.
  d Change 18 500 megawatts to terawatts.

7 The mass of a blue whale is 1.9×10^5 kg.
The mass of a house mouse is 1.9×10^{-2} kg.
How many times greater than the mass of the house mouse is the mass of the blue whale?

8 A bucket contains 1.5 kg of sand. A grain of sand weighs 1.9×10^{-5} g.
Work out the number of grains of sand in the bucket.
Give your answer correct to the nearest million.

9 Scientists estimate:
- there are about 100 billion galaxies in the observable universe and
- each galaxy contains an average of 300 billion stars.

Work out an estimate for the total number of stars in the observable universe.
Give your answer in standard form.
(1 billion = 10^9)

10 The table gives information about the number of litres of water used by a factory for seven days.

Monday	Tuesday	Wednesday	Thursday	Friday	Saturday	Sunday
9.32×10^5	9.85×10^5	1.02×10^6	9.93×10^5	1.18×10^6	1.05×10^6	9.66×10^5

Work out the mean amount of water the factory uses each day.
Give your answer in litres, in standard form.

11 $x = 4.5 \times 10^4$
For each of the following, give your answer in standard form correct to four decimal places.
  a Work out
    i x^3 **ii** $\sqrt[3]{x}$ **iii** $\frac{1}{x}$.
  b What number is half way between x and $\sqrt{x}$?

Number Strand 2 Using our number system Unit 7 Calculating with standard form

PB **ES** **12** The speed of light is approximately 3×10^8 m/s and the distance of the Earth from the Sun is approximately 1.5×10^{11} m.
Approximately how many seconds does it take for light to travel from the Sun to the Earth?

PB **ES** **13** The diagram shows the dimensions of a football pitch.

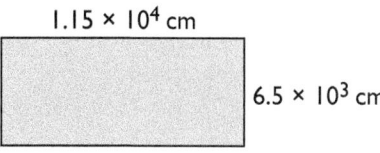

Work out

a the perimeter of the pitch

b the area of the pitch.

Give your answers in centimetres, in standard form.

PB **ES** **14** The diagram shows a circle drawn inside a square.

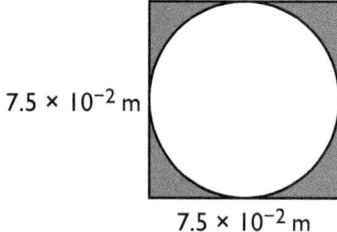

Work out the area, in m², of the dark shaded part.
Give your answer in standard form correct to 3 significant figures.

PB **ES** **15** The diagram shows a swimming pool in the shape of a prism.
The cross-section of the prism is a trapezium.
Work out the amount of water, in litres, in the swimming pool when it is full.
Give your answer in standard form correct to 3 significant figures.
(1 litre = 1000 cm³)

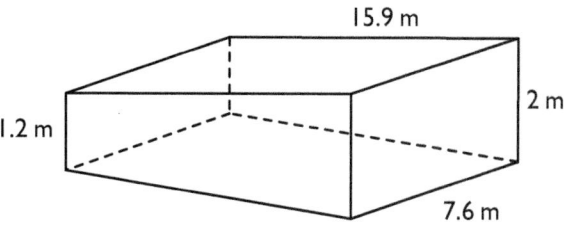

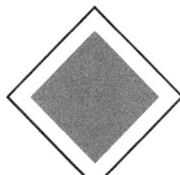

Number Strand 3 Accuracy
Unit 7 Limits of accuracy

PS PRACTISING SKILLS **DF** DEVELOPING FLUENCY **PB** PROBLEM SOLVING **ES** EXAM-STYLE

PS 1 Write down the lower and upper bounds for each of these measurements.

   a 2300 m (to the nearest m)
   b 2300 m (to the nearest 10 m)
   c 2300 m (to the nearest 100 m)
   d 2300 m (to the nearest 5 m)
   e 2300 m (to the nearest 50 m)

PS 2 Each of these measurements is rounded to the number of decimal places given in brackets.
Write down the lower and upper bounds for each measurement.

   a 7.8 ml (to 1 decimal place)
   b 0.3 ml (to 1 decimal place)
   c 0.07 ml (to 2 decimal places)
   d 3.88 m (to 2 decimal places)
   e 0.31 m (to 2 decimal places)
   f 0.058 m (to 3 decimal places)

PS 3 Each of these measurements is rounded to the given number of significant figures.
Write down the lower and upper bounds for each measurement.

   a 9 g (to 1 significant figure)
   b 90 g (to 1 significant figure)
   c 900 g (to 1 significant figure)
   d 8.4 cm (to 2 significant figures)
   e 84 cm (to 2 significant figures)
   f 0.84 cm (to 2 significant figures)

Number Strand 3 Accuracy Unit 7 Limits of accuracy

4 Copy and complete the inequality statement for each part.

  a The length of a ladder is x cm. To the nearest 10 cm, the length is 370 cm.
  $\boxed{} \leq x < \boxed{}$

  b The mass of an egg is m g. To the nearest gram, the mass is 57 g.
  $\boxed{} \leq m < \boxed{}$

  c The body temperature of a baby is T °C. To 1 decimal place, the temperature is 36.4 °C.
  $\boxed{} \leq T < \boxed{}$

  d The capacity of a saucepan is y litres. To 2 significant figures, the capacity is 2.8 litres.
  $\boxed{} \leq y < \boxed{}$

5 a Write $q = 3450$ (to the nearest 50) in the form $c \leq q < d$, where c and d are numbers to be found.

  b Write $95 \leq p < 105$ in the form $p \pm a$, where p and a are numbers to be found.

  c Write n (to the nearest 10) in the form $n \pm b$, where n and b are numbers to be found.

6 $x = 56.7$ (to 1 decimal place) and $y = 84.2$ (to 1 decimal place).

  a Work out the lower bound for x.

  b Work out the lower bound for y.

  c Work out the lower bound for $x + y$.

7 The table gives information about the daily water consumption for each member of the Jones family.

Name	Daily water consumption (to the nearest 5 gallons)
John	45
Mary	50
Chelsea	65
Brett	40

Work out

  a the lower bound

  b the upper bound

for the total daily water consumption of the Jones family.

8 A square field has side length 65 m, to the nearest metre. Work out the lower and upper bounds for

  a the perimeter of the square

  b the area of the square.

9 Given that $23.5 \leq l < 24.5$ and $17.5 \leq m < 18.5$, work out the upper bound for $l - m$.

10 A stadium sells premium tickets and standard tickets.
The cost of a premium ticket is £25.00.
The cost of a standard ticket is £12.50.
On Saturday:
- 2500 people buy a premium ticket (to the nearest 100)
- 7400 people buy a standard ticket (to the nearest 100).

Let T be the total amount of money paid for premium tickets and standard tickets.
Work out the lower bound and the upper bound for T.

11 Jim is reading a book. Each day, he reads 15 pages of the book (to the nearest 4 pages).
There are 281 pages in the book.
Jim thinks he will definitely finish the book in 3 weeks.
Is he right?
Show how you get your answer.

12 Helen recorded the time taken, to the nearest 10 seconds, for a cashier to serve each of four customers in a shop.
Here are her results.
150   220   190   110
Work out the lower bound for the mean time taken to serve these customers.

13 The diagram shows a badge that is in the shape of a sector of a circle.
The radius of the sector of the circle is 8.6 cm (to 2 significant figures).
Work out

a the upper bound for the perimeter of the badge

b the lower bound for the area of the badge.

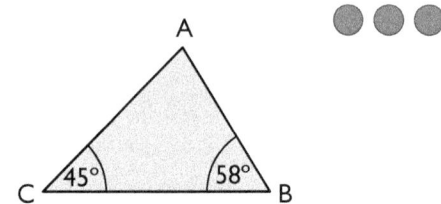

14 In this triangle:
Angle ACB = 45° (to the nearest degree)
Angle ABC = 58° (to the nearest degree)
Work out the upper bound for the size of the angle CAB.

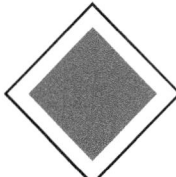

Number Strand 5 Percentages
Unit 6 Reverse percentages

PS PRACTISING SKILLS **DF** DEVELOPING FLUENCY **PB** PROBLEM SOLVING **ES** EXAM-STYLE

PS 1 A washing machine costs £270 which includes VAT at 20%.
Work out the cost of the washing machine without VAT.

PS 2 A computer costs £450 following a reduction of 25%.
Work out the cost of the computer before the reduction.

PS 3 8717 people visited a tourist attraction in June.
This is a 15% increase in the number of people who visited the attraction in May.
How many people visited the attraction in May?

PS 4 The cost of a barrel of oil at Toby's garage is £45. This is 60% less than it was 5 years ago.
Work out the cost of a barrel of oil at Toby's garage 5 years ago.

PS 5 A special bottle of Mega Juice contains 1.625 litres of orange juice.
This is 30% more than a standard bottle of Mega Juice.
Work out the amount of orange juice in a standard bottle of Mega Juice.

PS 6 The length of an iron rail at 30°C is 556.2 cm. This is 3% greater than the length of the iron rail at 10°C.
Work out the length of the iron rail at 10°C.

PS 7 The installation of a contactless ticket machine at a cinema reduces the average time taken to buy a film ticket by 28%. The average time taken to buy a film ticket using the contactless ticket machine is 153 seconds.
What was the average time taken to buy a film ticket before the installation of the contactless ticket machine?

DF 8 A sofa costs £840 which includes VAT at 20%.
Work out the VAT.

DF 9 Work out the original value for each of these.
   a ☐ cm is increased by 25% to give 107.5 cm.
   b ☐ g is decreased by 5% to give 461.51 g.
   c £☐ is increased by 36.5% to give £352.17.
   d ☐ litres is decreased by 17.5% to give 80.85 litres.
   e ☐ km is increased by 0.75% to give 39.091 km.

7

Number Strand 5 Percentages Unit 6 Reverse percentages

DF **10** Tony buys a suit, a shirt and a tie in a department store sale.
The price of the suit was reduced by 25% to £81.
The price of the shirt was reduced by 20% to £24.
The price of the tie was reduced by 75% to £5.
   a What was the price of the suit, the shirt and the tie before the sale?
   b How much money did Tony save?

DF **ES** **11** After a dry summer, Kings' Reservoir contained 1.5×10^{10} litres of water. This is 36% less than the maximum capacity of the reservoir.
Work out the maximum capacity of Kings' Reservoir.
Give your answer in standard form.

PB **ES** **12** Wendy worked for 20 hours in her part-time job this week.
This was an increase of $33\frac{1}{3}\%$ in the number of hours she worked last week.
Wendy is paid the same amount each hour.
This week Wendy's pay is £144.80. This was more than her pay last week.
How much more?

PB **ES** **13** The handbook of a motorbike states that the pressure, in pounds per square inch (psi), of the back tyre of the motorbike should be:
   • in the range 40.5–45 psi
   • 12.5% greater than the pressure of the front tyre of the motorbike.
Work out the range of possible pressures for the front tyre of the motorbike.

DF **14** Poppy recorded the times taken by some students to complete a Sudoku puzzle. Here are her results for the male students.
   12 min 18 sec   15 min 25 sec   14 min 5 sec   18 min 43 sec   16 min 55 sec
   17 min 47 sec   14 min 50 sec   13 min 29 sec   15 min 18 sec   16 min 22 sec
The mean time taken by the male students is 4% less than the mean time taken by the female students.
Work out the mean time taken by the female students.

PB **ES** **15** There are three heptagons, A, B and C.
The area of C is 30% greater than the area of B.
The area of B is 20% greater than the area of A.
The area of C is 70.2 cm².
Work out the area of A.

PB **16** 100 people watched the first round of a darts competition.
122 people watched the second round of the darts competition.
The number of males watching the second round was 20% greater than the number of males watching the first round.
The number of females watching the second round was 25% greater than the number of females watching the first round.
Work out the number of female spectators watching the second round of the competition.

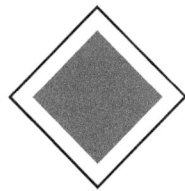

Number Strand 5 Percentages
Unit 7 Repeated percentage increase/decrease

PS — PRACTISING SKILLS   **DF** — DEVELOPING FLUENCY   **PB** — PROBLEM SOLVING   **ES** — EXAM-STYLE

PS 1 Write down the meaning of each calculation. The first one has been done for you.
  a 280 × 1.2   *Increase 280 by 20%.*
  b 280 × 1.25
  c 280 × 1.02
  d 280 × 1.025
  e 280 × 0.8
  f 280 × 0.85

PS 2 Copy and complete the calculation to work out each percentage change.
  a Increase 34.5 by 10%.   34.5 × ☐
  b Increase 12.45 by 17.5%.   12.45 × ☐
  c Increase 156.78 by 8%.   156.78 × ☐
  d Decrease 304 by 12%.   304 × ☐
  e Decrease 3.125 by 12.5%.   3.125 × ☐
  f Decrease 0.758 by 6.5%.   0.758 × ☐

PS 3 Calculate each of these.
  a Increase 400 by 10%. Increase the result by 10%.
  b i Increase 520 by 10%. Decrease the result by 10%.
     ii Explain why the answer is not 520.
  c Decrease 1200 by 15%. Increase the result by 20%.
  d Decrease 1840 by 25%. Decrease the result by 15%.

Number Strand 5 Percentages Unit 7 Repeated percentage increase/decrease

4 Ella invests £5000 into a bank account for 3 years. The bank pays compound interest at an annual rate of 5%.

Which calculation represents the value of the investment after 3 years?

a $5000 \times (0.05)^3$

b $5000 \times 0.05 \times 3$

c $5000 \times (1.05)^3$

d $5000 \times 1.05 \times 3$

5 Here is a number machine.

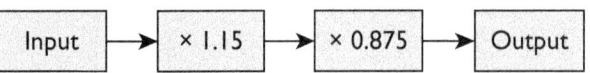

a Copy and complete the table for this number machine.

Input	520	0.8	108.8	2116
Output				

b What does the number machine do to an input number? Give your answer in terms of percentages.

6 The table gives some information about the number of seals on an island each April from 2010 to 2013.

Year	April 2010	April 2011	April 2012	April 2013
Percentage change	No information for previous year	10% more than previous year	7.5% less than previous year	5% more than previous year
Number of seals	8000			

Copy and complete the table.

7 Gemma invests £4000 for 3 years. The investment pays compound interest at an annual rate of 2%.

Harry invests £3800 for 3 years. His investment pays compound interest at an annual rate of 3%.

The total amount of interest that Harry gets for his investment is more than the total amount of interest that Gemma gets for her investment.

How much more?

10

Number Strand 5 Percentages Unit 7 Repeated percentage increase/decrease

8 The picture shows three statues.

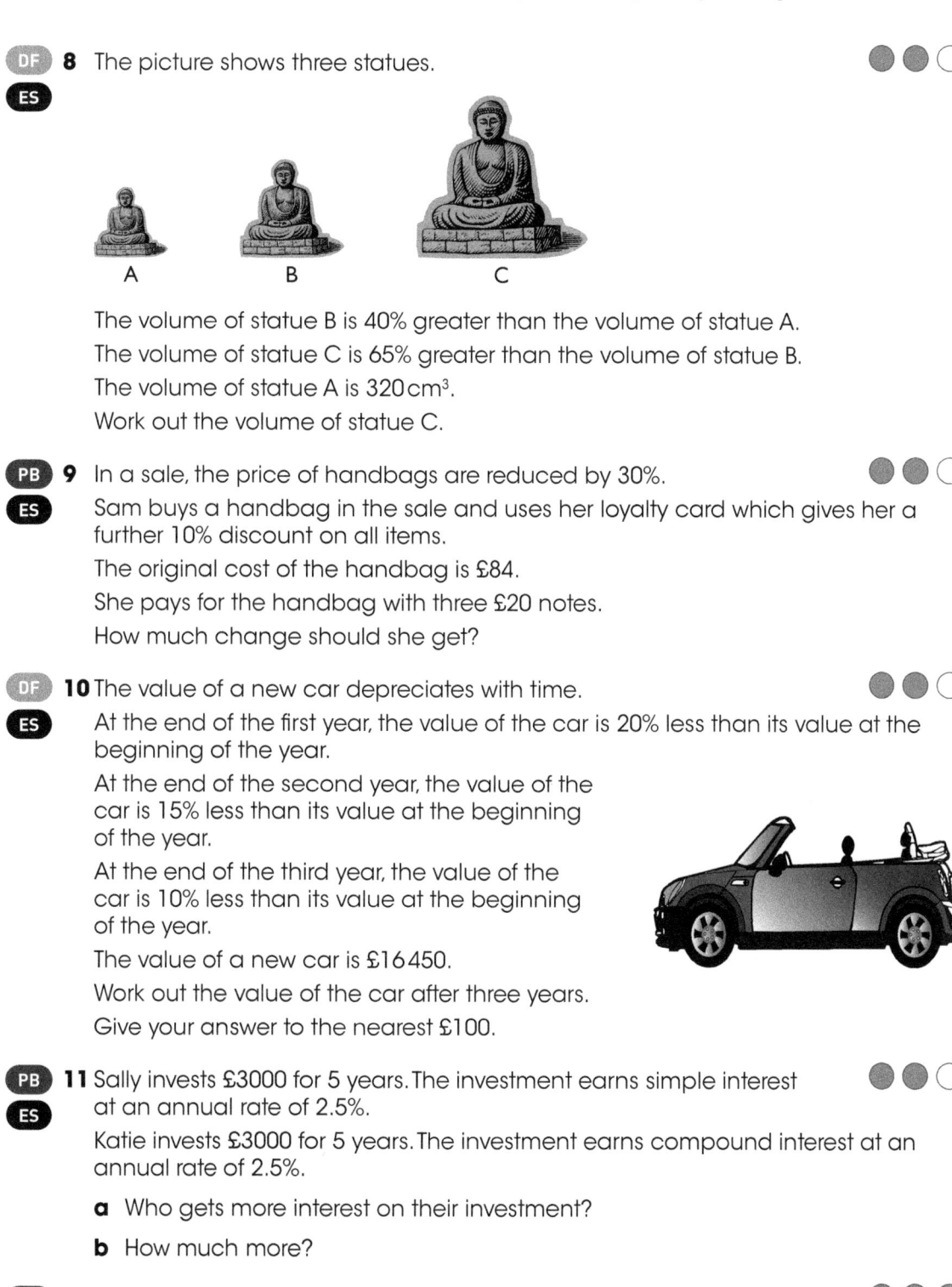

A   B   C

The volume of statue B is 40% greater than the volume of statue A.
The volume of statue C is 65% greater than the volume of statue B.
The volume of statue A is 320 cm³.
Work out the volume of statue C.

9 In a sale, the price of handbags are reduced by 30%.
Sam buys a handbag in the sale and uses her loyalty card which gives her a further 10% discount on all items.
The original cost of the handbag is £84.
She pays for the handbag with three £20 notes.
How much change should she get?

10 The value of a new car depreciates with time.
At the end of the first year, the value of the car is 20% less than its value at the beginning of the year.
At the end of the second year, the value of the car is 15% less than its value at the beginning of the year.
At the end of the third year, the value of the car is 10% less than its value at the beginning of the year.
The value of a new car is £16 450.
Work out the value of the car after three years.
Give your answer to the nearest £100.

11 Sally invests £3000 for 5 years. The investment earns simple interest at an annual rate of 2.5%.
Katie invests £3000 for 5 years. The investment earns compound interest at an annual rate of 2.5%.

   a Who gets more interest on their investment?
   b How much more?

12 Clio plants a tree that is 2 m in height.
The height of the tree increases by 10% each year.
How many years will it take for the tree to reach a height of 4 m?

Number Strand 6 Ratio and proportion Unit 4 The constant of proportionality

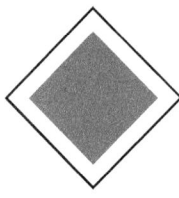

PS PRACTISING SKILLS   **DF** DEVELOPING FLUENCY   **PB** PROBLEM SOLVING   **ES** EXAM-STYLE

PS 1 y is proportional to x.
When $x = 8$, $y = 5$.
  a Write down a formula involving a constant k that connects y and x.
  b Work out the value of y when $x = 12$.
  c Work out the value of x when $y = 16$.

PS 2 The graph shows information about the variables P and w.

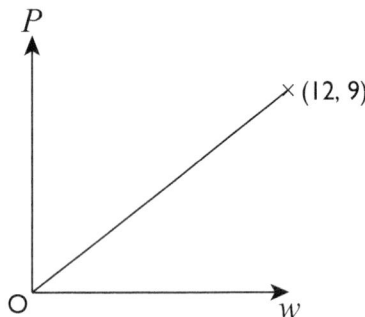

Write down a formula connecting P and w.

PS 3 V is directly proportional to n. The constant of proportionality is 2.25.
Copy and complete the table of values.

n	3	5		12	
V	6.75		15.75		72

PS 4 S is directly proportional to T. When $T = 10$, $S = 120$.
  a Draw the graph of S for $0 \leq T \leq 10$.
  b Write down a formula connecting S and T.

5 Graham records the values of a variable c for different values of a second variable h.

The table shows his results.

h	2	6	15
c	3	8	20

Graham says, 'c is directly proportional to h'.
Is Graham correct? Give a reason for your answer.

6 The circumference (C) of a circle is directly proportional to its diameter (d).
The graph shows the relationship between C and d.

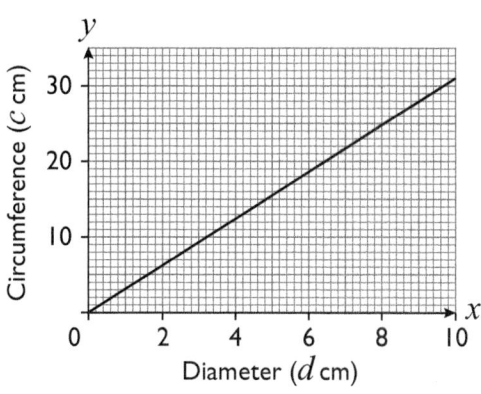

$C = kd$

a Use the graph to find the approximate value of the constant of proportionality k.

b What does the value of k represent in this case?

7 $A = kx$
When $x = 16, A = 4$.

a Work out the value of k.

b $B = 1.5x$ and $Y = A + B$

Copy and complete the table of values for $x = 4, x = 8, x = 12$ and $x = 16$.

x	4	8	12	16
A		2		4
B	6			24
$Y = A + B$	7			28

c Explain why Y is directly proportional to x.

d Write down a formula connecting Y and x.

8 K (kilometres) α M (miles)

16 kilometres = 10 miles

a Write a formula connecting K and M.

b Michael walks 19 kilometres. Sarah walks 12 miles.
Who walked the greater distance, and by how much?

9 The cost of waxing a floor, £C, is directly proportional to the area, a m², of the floor.

Tracey waxes the floor in her living room. It cost her £350 to wax an area of 28 m².

a Write a formula connecting C and a.

b What does the value of the constant of proportionality represent in your formula?

c The diagram shows the floor plan for Tracey's dining room.
She has saved £150. Will this be enough to wax her dining room floor?

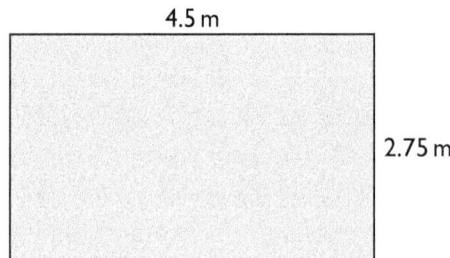

4.5 m

2.75 m

10 Larry drives his van at a constant speed.
At this constant speed:
- the cost of fuel, £C, is directly proportional to the distance travelled, d km
- the distance travelled, d km, is directly proportional to the length of time, t hours, Larry is travelling.

When d = 47.5 km, C = £2.85.
When t = 4.8 hours, d = 210 km.

a Work out the value of C when t = 1.6 hours.

b Work out the value of t when C = £50.

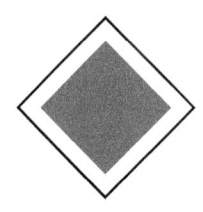

Number Strand 6 Ratio and proportion Unit 5 Working with inversely proportional quantities

PS — PRACTISING SKILLS   **DF** — DEVELOPING FLUENCY   **PB** — PROBLEM SOLVING   **ES** — EXAM-STYLE

PS 1 $h = \dfrac{225}{p}$

Work out the value of h when

a $p = 9$

b $p = 45$.

PS 2 $PV = k$, where k is a constant.
When $V = 10$, $P = 9$.

a Work out the value of k.

b Work out the value of P when $V = 5$.

c Work out the value of V when $P = 15$.

PS 3 For each table of values, state whether (or not) the two variables are in inverse proportion.

a

x	45	60	90	180
y	8	6	4	2

b

x	6	10	15	42
P	35	21	14	5

c

t	2	3	5	7
S	26	39	65	91

d

V	3	15	65	273
R	455	91	21	5

4 $y = \dfrac{k}{x}$, where k is a constant.

    a Copy and complete these statements.
        i y is _____ proportional to _____.
        ii k is the _____.

    b When $x = 5$, $y = 20$.
       Work out the value of k.

    c Work out the value of y when $x = 12.5$.

    d Work out the value of x when $y = 25$.

5 The graph shows V against x.

    a Copy the table and complete it using the information in the graph.

x	1	2			6	10
V	30		10	5		

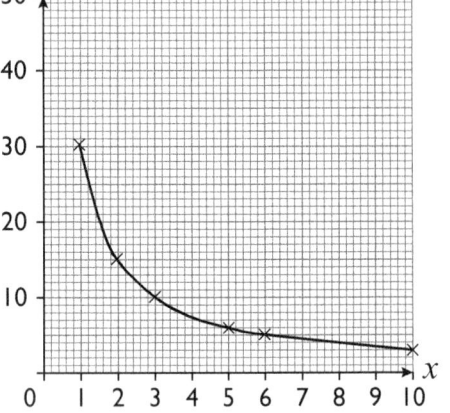

    b Explain why V is inversely proportional to x.

    c Write down a formula connecting V and x.

    d Work out the value of V when
        i $x = 4$
        ii $x = 100$.

    e Work out the value of x when
        i $V = 45$
        ii $V = 150$.

6 For a constant mass of metal, the density, d g/cm³, is inversely proportional to the volume, V cm³.

The table gives information about the densities and the volumes of 1 kg of some common metals. All measurements are correct to 3 significant figures.

Metal	Gold	Silver	Lead	Copper	Iron	Platinum
Density d g/cm³	19.3	10.5	11.3	8.96	7.87	21.5
Volume, V cm³	51.8	95.2	88.5	112.0	127.0	46.5

    a Draw a graph of V against d.

    b Write down a formula connecting V and d for 1 kg of a metal.

    c The density of mercury is 13.5 g/cm³. Work out the volume of 1 kg of mercury.

Number Strand 6 Ratio and proportion Unit 5 Working with inversely proportional quantities

7 The volume (V) of a gas is inversely proportional to the pressure (P) at constant temperature.
There is 10000 cm³ of neon gas in a balloon at a pressure of 1.5 atmospheres.
Work out the volume of neon gas in the balloon when the pressure is increased to 2 atmospheres. Assume the temperature is constant.

8 The cost of the labour to build a patio is £600.
The table gives some information about the hourly rate, £R, and the time taken, t hours, to build the patio.

t	25	40	50	60	75
R	24	15	12	10	8

a Write down a formula connecting R and t.
b Work out the hourly rate when it takes 30 hours to build the patio.
c Work out the time taken to build the patio for an hourly rate of £12.50.

9 The length, y m, and the width, x m, of the rectangle are variables.
The area, A m², of the rectangle is 3990
Work out the perimeter of the rectangle when $x = 38$

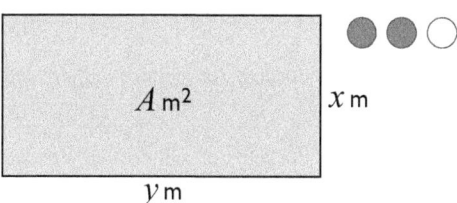

10 Kerry is putting some washers into bags. She puts the same number of washers into each bag.
The number of washers, w, she puts into each bag is inversely proportional to the number of bags, p, she uses.

a Copy and complete the table of values.

Number of washers in each bag, w	15	30		45
Number of bags, p	42		18	

b Kerry puts 21 of these washers into each bag. A bag costs 5p.
Work out the total cost of the bags.

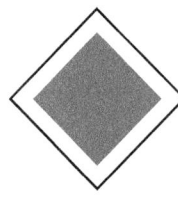

Number Strand 7 Number properties Unit 4 Index notation

PS PRACTISING SKILLS   **DF** DEVELOPING FLUENCY   **PB** PROBLEM SOLVING   **ES** EXAM-STYLE

PS 1 Write each of these as a power of 2.
  a $2 \times 2 \times 2$
  b $2 \times 2 \times 2 \times 2 \times 2 \times 2 \times 2 \times 2 \times 2$
  c $(2 \times 2 \times 2 \times 2) \times (2 \times 2)$
  d $(2 \times 2) \times (2 \times 2) \times (2 \times 2)$

PS 2 Change $1\,m^2$ to mm^2.
ES Give your answer as a single power of 10.

PS 3 Write each of these as a power of 3.
  a $\dfrac{3 \times 3 \times 3}{3}$
  b $\dfrac{3 \times 3 \times 3 \times 3 \times 3}{3 \times 3}$
  c $\dfrac{3 \times 3 \times 3 \times 3 \times 3 \times 3 \times 3}{3 \times 3 \times 3}$
  d $\dfrac{(3 \times 3 \times 3 \times 3 \times 3) \times (3 \times 3 \times 3)}{3 \times (3 \times 3 \times 3)}$

PS 4 Write each of these in index form.
  a $(2 \times 2 \times 2 \times 2) \div (2 \times 2)$
  b $(5 \times 5 \times 5 \times 5 \times 5) \div (5 \times 5 \times 5)$
  c $(7 \times 7 \times 7 \times 7 \times 7) \div (7 \times 7)$
  d $(11 \times 11 \times 11) \div (11 \times 11)$

PS 5 Write each of these as a single power of 3.
  a $3^2 \times 3^3$
  b $3 \times 3^2 \times 3^3$
  c $27 \times 9 \times 81$

PS 6 Write each of these as a single power of 5.
  a $5^4 \div 5^2$
  b $5^4 \div 5$
  c $5^5 \div 125$

PS 7 Write each of these in index form.
  a $2 \times 2 \times 2 \times 3 \times 3$
  b $2 \times 3 \times 2 \times 2 \times 2 \times 3$
  c $5 \times 7 \times 7 \times 7 \times 7 \times 7 \times 5$
  d $3 \times 3 \times 2 \times 5 \times 2 \times 5 \times 2 \times 5$

Number Strand 7 Number properties Unit 4 Index notation

8 Write each of these as a single power of 2.
  a 4^2 b 8^2 c 16^2

9 Work out the area of each shape. Give your answers in index form.

a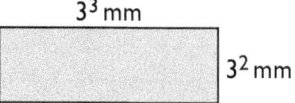

b

c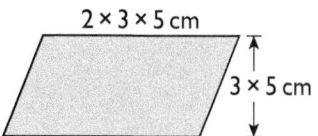

d (rectangle 32 cm by 16 cm)

10 Simplify each of these. Give your answers in index form.
  a $(3^2)^2$ b $(5^3)^2$ c $(2^2)^3$ d $(11^4)^2$

11 Simplify each of these. Give your answers in index form.
  a $\dfrac{3^7}{3^2 \times 3^3}$ b $\dfrac{7^5 \times 7^3}{7^3 \times 7^2}$ c $\dfrac{5^3 \times 5^2}{5^3 \div 5^2}$ d $\dfrac{(2^4)^2}{2^3}$ e $\dfrac{(3^3)^3}{(3^2)^3}$

12 There are 64 squares on a chessboard.

Milo is going to put 1 grain of barley on the first square of the chessboard, 2 grains on the second square, 4 grains on the third square, 8 grains on the fourth square, and so on.

16 grains of barley weigh 1 g. Work out the total mass of the barley on the 64th square of the chessboard.

Give your answer in kilograms, in standard form and correct to 3 significant figures.

13 a Write 125 as a power of 5.
  b Show that $125^2 = 25^3$, without the use of a calculator.

14 You are given that
  $x = 3 \times 5^3$
  $y = 2 \times 5^2$ and
  $x + 5y = 5^n$, where n is an integer.
Work out the value of n.

15 The formula $P = 2^n - 1$, where n is a prime number, is used to find prime numbers (P).
Can the formula be used to find all possible prime numbers?
Give a reason for your answer.

19

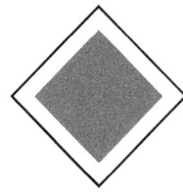

Number Strand 7 Number properties Unit 5 Prime factorisation

PS PRACTISING SKILLS   **DF** DEVELOPING FLUENCY   **PB** PROBLEM SOLVING   **ES** EXAM-STYLE

PS 1 Write each of these in index form.

a $3 \times 3 \times 2$
b $5 \times 3 \times 5 \times 5$
c $5 \times 7 \times 5 \times 7$
d $2 \times 5 \times 3 \times 5 \times 2$
e $3 \times 2 \times 3 \times 2 \times 3$
f $2 \times 7 \times 2 \times 2 \times 7$
g $3 \times 5 \times 3 \times 2 \times 3 \times 5$
h $2 \times 5 \times 2 \times 5 \times 2 \times 2$
i $5 \times 3 \times 5 \times 3 \times 5 \times 2$

PS 2 Here are some numbers given as products of their prime factors. Write the numbers in order of size, starting with the smallest.

2×7^2 $2^2 \times 3 \times 5$ $2 \times 3 \times 11$ $2^3 \times 3^2$

DF 3 Write each number as a product of its prime factors in index form.

a 105   b 165   c 315   d 150
e 525   f 36   g 225   h 588

PS 4 Copy and complete the table.

Numbers	Factors	Common factors	Highest common factor, HCF
15, 20	15: 1, 3, 5, 15 20: 1, 2, 4, 5, 10, 20	1, 5	5
8, 28	8: 1, 2, 4, 8 28: 1, 2, 4, 7, 14, 28	1, 2, 4	
16, 40	16: 1, 2, 4, 8, 16 40: 1, 2, 4, 5, 8, 10, 20, 40		
24, 36			

PS 5 Find the HCF of each pair of numbers.

a 18 and 30   b 27 and 36   c 28 and 70   d 52 and 130
e 36 and 54   f 24 and 60   g 42 and 63   h 72 and 120

Number Strand 7 Number properties Unit 5 Prime factorisation

PS 6 Here are the first 12 multiples of 5 and 6.
Multiples of 5   5 10 15 20 25 30 35 40 45 50 55 60
Multiples of 6   6 12 18 24 30 36 42 48 54 60 66 72

  a Which numbers are multiples of both 5 and 6?
  b Write down the lowest common multiple (LCM) of 5 and 6.

PS 7 Write down the LCM of each pair.
  a 6 and 7   **b** 10 and 15   **c** 8 and 12   **d** 9 and 12
  e 90 and 135   **f** 15 and 50   **g** 24 and 40   **h** 18 and 48

DF 8 Copy and complete these statements.
  a $2 \times 5 \times 7^2 = \boxed{}$
  b $3 \times 5^2 \times \boxed{} = 825$
  c $2 \times 3^{\boxed{}} \times 5 = 90$
  d $2 \times 3 \times \boxed{}^2 = 294$
  e $2^3 \times \boxed{}^2 = 200$
  f $2^2 \times 3^{\boxed{}} \times 5^2 = 2700$

DF 9 Match two letter cards with each HCF card.

A	B	C	D	HCF	HCF
9	12	15	18	3	6

DF 10 $30 = 2 \times 3 \times 5$ and $105 = 3 \times 5 \times 7$

  a Which prime factors are common to 30 and 105?
  b Copy and complete the Venn diagram.

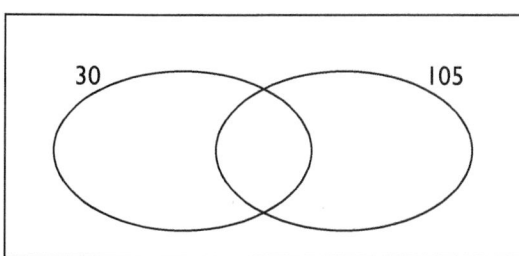

  c Write down the HCF of 30 and 105.

DF 11 a Write 126 as a product of its prime factors.
  b Write 180 as a product of its prime factors.
  c Draw a Venn diagram to show the prime factors of 126 and 180.
  d Write down the HCF of 126 and 180.

Number Strand 7 Number properties Unit 5 Prime factorisation

12 The table shows the quantities and costs of pencils and erasers.

	Pencils	Erasers
Number in a box	8	10
Cost	£1.80	£2.40

Simon wants to buy as many pencils and erasers as possible, but he wants to buy exactly the same number of each. He has £40.

Work out the total cost of pencils and erasers that Simon should buy.

13 The diagram shows three lighthouses, A, B and C.

The lights on lighthouse A flash once every 5 seconds.
The lights on lighthouse B flash once every 7 seconds.
The lights on lighthouse C flash once every 15 seconds.
Peter is standing on an island watching the lighthouses.
At 21:00, all three lighthouses flash together.
How many times will all three lighthouses flash together during the next hour?

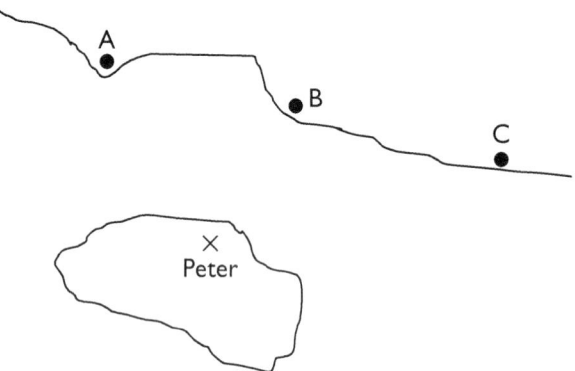

14 The diagram shows two cogs, X and Y. An arrow is drawn on each cog.
Cog X has 10 teeth.
Cog Y has 12 teeth.
Cog X is turned in a clockwise direction until the arrows return to their starting positions.
Work out the angle through which cog X is turned.

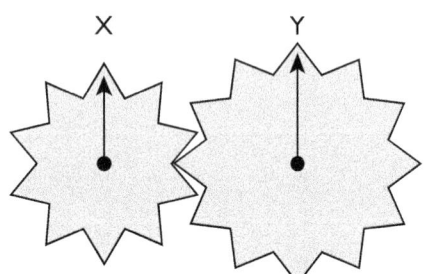

Number Strand 7 Number properties Unit 6 Rules of indices

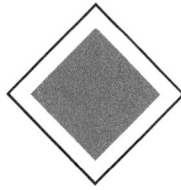

PS – PRACTISING SKILLS   **DF** – DEVELOPING FLUENCY   **PB** – PROBLEM SOLVING   **ES** – EXAM-STYLE

PS 1 Copy and complete the table by writing each number as a single power of 5.

Ordinary number	125	25	5	1	$\frac{1}{5}$	$\frac{1}{25}$	$\frac{1}{125}$
Index form		5^2					

PS 2 Use the rule $a^n \times a^m = a^{n+m}$ to simplify each of these. Give your answers in index form.

a $2^3 \times 2^4$

b $7^2 \times 7^3$

c $2^{-2} \times 2^{-5}$

d $2^{-1} \times 2^5$

e $7^3 \times 7^0$

PS 3 Use the rule $a^n \div a^m = a^{n-m}$ to simplify each of these. Give your answers in index form.

a $5^7 \div 5^6$

b $\dfrac{3^6}{3^8}$

c $2^3 \div 2^{-3}$

d $7^{-1} \div 7^{-1}$

e $\dfrac{11^{-2}}{11^8}$

PS 4 Use the rule $(a^m)^n = a^{m \times n}$ to simplify each of these. Give your answers in index form.

a $(5^2)^3$

b $(2^5)^3$

c $(7^3)^{-2}$

d $(2^5)^0$

e $(11^{-3})^{-2}$

23

Number Strand 7 Number properties Unit 6 Rules of indices

PS 5 Write each of these as a fraction in its simplest form.
For example, $2^{-3} = \frac{1}{2^3} = \frac{1}{8}$.

    a 2^{-2} **b** 3^{-2} **c** 11^{-1} **d** 10^{-3}

DF 6 Without using a calculator, state which of these is equal to 1.

    a 5^0 **b** $3^2 \times 3^{-2}$ **c** $(5^3)^{-2}$ **d** $2^5 \div 2^5$ **e** $(7^3)^0$

DF 7 Write each of these as a single power of 2.

    a 4   **b** 4^2 **c** $(4^3)^2$ **d** $(4^5)^4$

DF 8 Work out each of these. Give your answers in index form.

    a $(2^2 \times 2^3) \times 2^4$

    b $(7^3 \times 7^4) \div 7^5$

    c $(5^8 \div 5^5) \times 5^2$

    d $(2^8 \div 2^5) \times (2^7 \div 2^2)$

    e $(3^2 \times 3^6) \div (3^5 \times 3^2)$

    f $(2^3)^2 \times (2^2)^3$

    g $(5^4 \div 5^6)^{-1}$

DF 9 $3^4 = 81$ and $3^5 = 243$

Write the answer to each of these as a single power of 3. Do not use a calculator.

    a 9×81

    b 27×243^2

    c $\dfrac{243}{9}$

    d $\dfrac{9}{243}$

    e $\dfrac{243 \times 81^2}{27}$

DF 10 Use the rules of indices to simplify each of these. Give your answers in index form.

    a $2^3 \times 2^4 \times 3^4 \times 3^2$

    b $5^2 \times 7^3 \times 5^3 \times 7^2$

    c $\dfrac{3^5 \times 5^4}{3^2 \times 5^2}$

    d $\dfrac{2^5 \times 2^4}{7^2 \times 7^8}$

    e $(2^5 \times 5^3)^2$

11 Without using a calculator, copy and complete these statements.
Use < or > or =.

a $2^3 \;\square\; 3^2$

b $(2^3)^2 \;\square\; (2^2)^3$

c $2^{-1} \;\square\; 3^{-1}$

d $3^0 \;\square\; 3$

e $\dfrac{2^{-1}}{2^{-2}} \;\square\; 2$

12 $5^3 = 125$ and $5^5 = 3125$

Pierre says $125^{10} = 3125^6$.

Without using a calculator, say whether or not he is correct. Explain why.

13 Damien says $(a^m)^n = (a^n)^m$.

Is he correct? Explain why.

14 Write down the HCF of each pair of numbers.

a 42 and 70

b 42^2 and 70^2

15 Show that $(2^a \times 2^b) \times 2^c = 2^b \times (2^a \times 2^c)$.

Algebra Strand 1 Starting algebra Unit 7 Working with more complex equations

1 Solve these equations.
   a $5 - 4x = 24$
   b $2a - 7 = 1 - 3a$

2 Alex and Josh try to solve this equation.
$8x - 5 = 2x + 10$

Alex's solution
$-5 - 10 = 2x - 8x$
$+15 = -6x$
$x = 15 \div -6 = -2.5$

Josh's solution
$8x - 2x = 10 + 5$
$6x = 15$
$x = 15 - 6 = 9$

   a Both Alex and Josh have made a mistake. Explain each boy's mistake.
   b Find the correct solution.

3 Jenny and Rhea need to solve this equation.
$5y + 13 = 1 - y$
Here is how they start.

Jenny
$5y + y = 1 - 13$
$6y = -12$
$y = \text{................}$

Rhea
$13 - 1 = -y - 5y$
$12 = -6y$
$y = \text{................}$

   a Complete their solutions.
   b Which method do you prefer? Explain why.

4 Bill pays £7.80 for 3 meat pies and 2 steak puddings.
Misha pays £12.60 for 7 meat pies.
Lisa pays £2.45 for 1 meat pie and 1 portion of chips.
Work out the cost of
   a 1 portion of chips
   b 1 steak pudding.

5 Anne and Brian collect football stickers.
There are x stickers in a full set of football stickers.
Anne has 3 full sets and 8 stickers. Brian has 1 full set and 32 stickers.
They each have the same number of stickers.
How many stickers are in a full set?

6 Here is a rectangle. All the measurements are in centimetres.
Work out the perimeter of this rectangle.

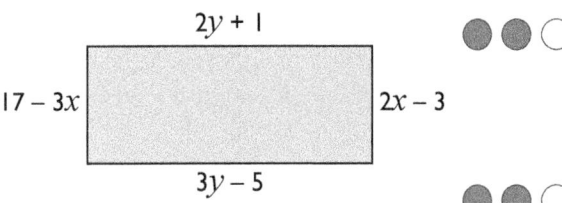

7 Tom is x years old.
Bronwyn is 4 times as old as Tom.
Tom is 5 years older than Pat.
In 12 years' time, Bronwyn will be 9 years older than the sum of Tom and Pat's ages.
How old was Pat last year?

8 Carriage E and carriage F are two carriages on a train.
At Birmingham, there are 37 people in carriage E and 40 people in carriage F.
At Stoke:
- Three times as many people leave carriage E as leave carriage F.
- 20 people get on the train and go into carriage E.
- 11 people get on the train and go into carriage F.

The number of people in carriage E is now the same as the number of people in carriage F.
How many people from carriage E got off the train at Stoke?

9 The diagram shows a square and an equilateral triangle. All measurements are in centimetres.
The perimeter of the square is equal to the perimeter of the equilateral triangle.
Work out the area of the square.

 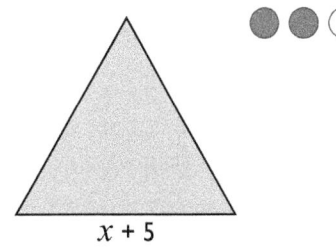

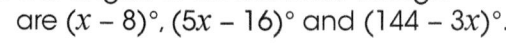

10 The angles of an isosceles triangle are $(x-8)°$, $(5x-16)°$ and $(144-3x)°$.
Work out the size of the smallest angle.

Algebra Strand 1 Starting algebra Unit 8 Solving equations with brackets

PS PRACTISING SKILLS **DF** DEVELOPING FLUENCY **PB** PROBLEM SOLVING **ES** EXAM-STYLE

PS ES 1 Solve these equations.
  a $3 - 2x = 3(x - 7)$
  b $1 - 2(a + 1) = 4(a - 5)$

DF ES 2 Toby is trying to solve this equation.
  $4x - 3 = 1 - (x - 4)$
  Here is his solution.

  $4x - 3 = 1 - x - 4$
  $4x + x = 1 - 4 + 3$
  $5x = -6$
  $x = -1.2$

  Toby has made two mistakes.
  Explain these mistakes.

PB ES 3 The length of this rectangle is twice the width.
  Work out the perimeter of the rectangle.

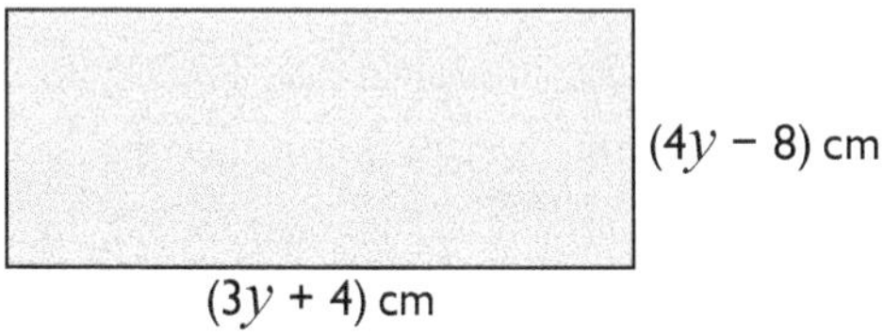

$(4y - 8)$ cm

$(3y + 4)$ cm

PB ES 4 A packet of crisps cost x pence.
  A can of cola costs 70p.
  Three boys each buy a packet of crisps and a can of cola.
  The total cost is £5.70.
  Martin wants to buy two cans of cola and a packet of crisps.
  How much will this cost?

PB ES 5 Ruby thinks of a number between 1 and 15.
  When she subtracts the number from 25 and then multiplies the result by 3, she gets the same answer as when she multiplies the number by 4 and then subtracts 9 from the result.
  What number is Ruby thinking of?

Algebra Strand 1 Starting algebra Unit 8 Solving equations with brackets

6 Tina is going to cover a floor with exactly 300 rectangular tiles like the one shown in the diagram.

There will be 15 rows with 20 tiles in each row.

The floor is in the shape of a rectangle with dimensions 2.4 m by 5 m.

What are the dimensions of each tile?

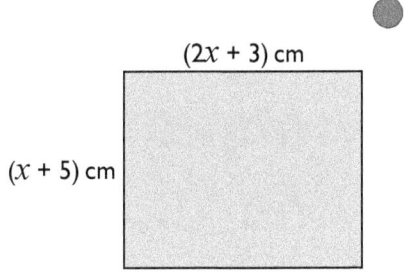

$(2x + 3)$ cm

$(x + 5)$ cm

7 When Zach was three years old, his height was h cm.

The table shows the increases in Zach's height over the next four years.

Age in years	3	4	5	6	7
Increase in height in cm		5	3	2	2

Zach's father is 1.80 metres tall.

When Zach was seven, he was half the height of his father.

Work out Zach's height when he was three.

8 In this isosceles triangle, the two equal angles are given by the expression $(x + 20)°$.

Show that the third angle can be written as $2(70 - x)°$.

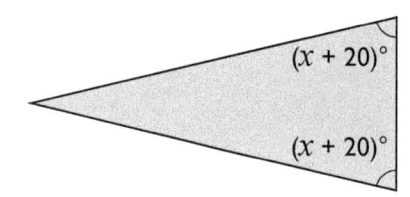

$(x + 20)°$

$(x + 20)°$

9 The radius of a circle is $(3x - 1)$ cm.

The circumference of the circle is equal to the perimeter of a square of side πx cm.

Show that the area of the circle can be written as 4π cm².

10 On the diagram, all measurements are in centimetres and all angles are right angles.

Show that the perimeter could never be equal to 32 cm.

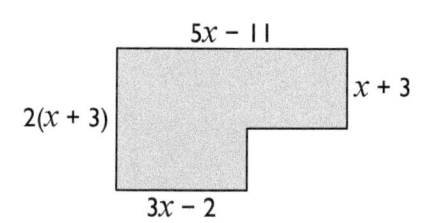

$5x - 11$

$x + 3$

$2(x + 3)$

$3x - 2$

29

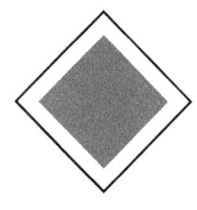

Algebra Strand 1 Starting algebra Unit 9 Simplifying harder expressions

PS — PRACTISING SKILLS   **DF** — DEVELOPING FLUENCY   **PB** — PROBLEM SOLVING   **ES** — EXAM-STYLE

PB **ES** **1** Waqar, Nathan and Wesley play for the school football team.
Waqar has scored 5 more goals than Nathan.
If Nathan scores another goal, he will have scored twice as many goals as Wesley.
Wesley has scored g goals. The three boys have scored a total of T goals.
Write down an expression for T in terms of g.

PB **2** Tom thinks of a number n and adds 4.
Jane thinks of a number m and subtracts 7.
Write down and expand an expression for the product of their results.

PB **ES** **3** Write down an expression, in terms of x, for the area of this shape.

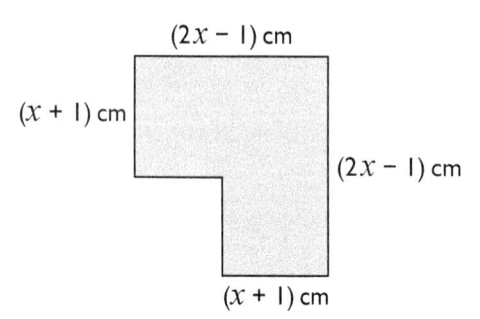

$(2x - 1)$ cm
$(x + 1)$ cm
$(2x - 1)$ cm
$(x + 1)$ cm

PB **ES** **4** The diagram shows a lawn in the shape of a square with a path around it.
The lawn is of side $(x + 3)$ m.
The width of the path is 1 m.
Write down an expression, in terms of x, for the total area of the path.

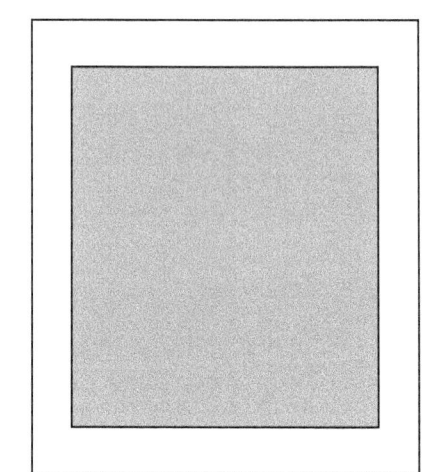

Algebra Strand 1 Starting algebra Unit 9 Simplifying harder expressions

5 The diagram shows a square and a right-angled triangle.
Show that the area of the square is never equal to the area of the right-angled triangle.

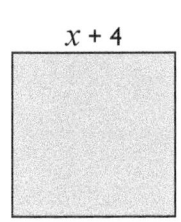

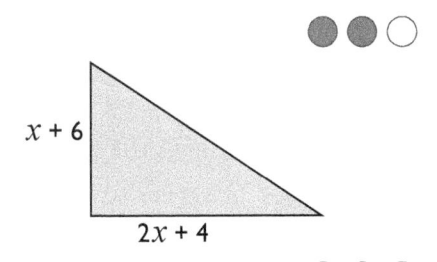

6 Show that the area of this trapezium is $x^2 - 16$.

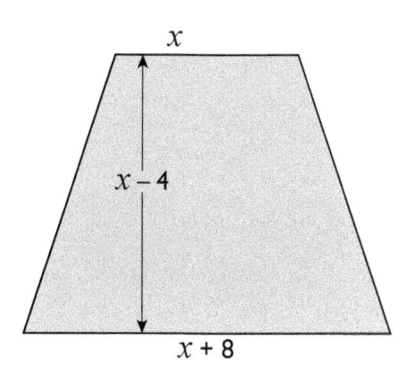

7 Write down in terms of x
   a the area of the shaded rectangle
   b the area of the shaded triangle.
   Expand and simplify your expressions, if necessary.

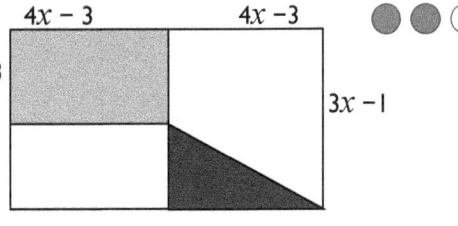

8 Here is a right-angled triangle.
Write down an expression for y in terms of x.

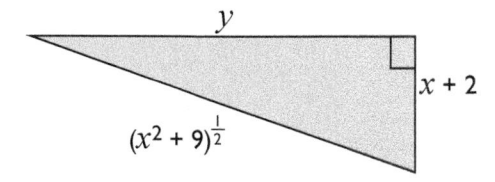

9 a Expand and simplify $(y - 5)(y + 8)$.
   b Simplify $\dfrac{(2w^2x)^3}{2w^3x \times 3wx^2}$.

10 $\left(x^{n+1}\right)^{n-1} = x^3$

For what value of n is this statement true?

31

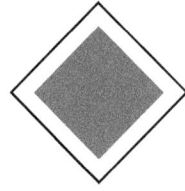

Algebra Strand 1 Starting algebra Unit 10 Using complex formulae

PS — PRACTISING SKILLS **DF** — DEVELOPING FLUENCY **PB** — PROBLEM SOLVING **ES** — EXAM-STYLE

DF ES 1 BB Cars uses the formula $C = 20 + 12.5Gt$ to work out the cost, $£C$, of renting a car, where G is the group of the car (1, 2, 3 or 4) and t is the number of days for which the car is rented.

Mary paid £370 to rent a car from BB Cars.

Work out one possibility for the number of days and the group of car that Mary rented.

PS ES 2 To change P pounds into E euros, Pete uses the formula $E = 1.36P$.

To change P pounds into D dollars, Pete uses the formula $D = 1.55P$.

   a Write down a formula that Pete could use to change dollars into euros.

   b Pete sees a watch for sale on an American website for 200 dollars.
The same model of watch is for sale in Spain for 175 euros.
In the UK, this model of watch is sold for 130 pounds.
In which currency is the watch cheapest?

PS ES 3 Here is a formula.

$v = u + at$

   a Work out the value of v when $u = 25$, $a = -10$ and $t = 3.5$.

   b Rearrange the formula to make a the subject.

   c Work out the value of a when $v = 80$, $u = 60$ and $t = 15$.

DF ES 4 The formula for calculating the volume (V) of a sphere is $V = \frac{4}{3}\pi r^3$, where r is the radius of the sphere.

   a Work out the volume of a sphere of radius 4.5 cm. Leave your answer in terms of π.

   b Work out the radius of a sphere of volume 200 mm³.

Algebra Strand 1 Starting algebra Unit 10 Using complex formulae

5 A can of cola is in the shape of a cylinder.
The volume of a cylinder (V) is given by the formula $V = \pi r^2 h$, where r is the radius and h is the height of the cylinder.
Peter buys a can that holds 330 ml of cola.
The radius of the can is 3.25 cm.
Work out the height of the can. Take $\pi = 3.14$.

6 The surface area (A) of a solid cylinder can be found using the formula $A = 2\pi r^2 + 2\pi r h$, where r is the radius of the cylinder and h is its height.

  a Work out the surface area of a cylinder with radius 7 cm and height 15 cm. Give your answer in terms of π.

  b Work out the height of a cylinder with surface area 20π and radius 2 cm.

7 Here is a formula.
$v^2 = u^2 + 2as$

  a Work out the value of v when $u = 20$, $a = 10$ and $s = 11.25$.

  b Rearrange the formula to make u the subject.

  c Work out the value of u when $v = 9$, $a = 4$ and $s = 7$.

8 The formula $T = 2\pi \sqrt{\dfrac{l}{g}}$ is used to calculate the time period, T, of a simple pendulum where l is the length in centimetres and g is the acceleration due to gravity.

  a Work out the value of T when $l = 160$ cm and $g = 10$ m/s². Give your answer in terms of π.

  b For another simple pendulum, $T = \dfrac{2\pi}{7}$.
  Work out the length of this simple pendulum when $g = 9.8$ m/s².

9 Here is a formula.
$c = \sqrt{a^2 + b^2}$

  a Make b the subject of the formula.

  b Work out the value of b when $c = 41$ and $a = 40$.

10 Here is a formula.
$E = mc^2$
Work out the value of

  a E when $m = 2 \times 10^{30}$ and $c = 3 \times 10^8$

  b m when $E = 4.5 \times 10^{28}$ and $c = 3 \times 10^8$.

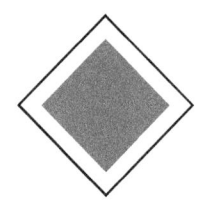

Algebra Strand 1 Starting algebra Unit 11 Identities

PS PRACTISING SKILLS   **DF** DEVELOPING FLUENCY   **PB** PROBLEM SOLVING   **ES** EXAM-STYLE

PS 1 Write down whether each statement is an identity (I), an equation (Q), an expression (X) or a formula (F).

  a $m^2 + 5m + 6 = 0$
  b $m^2 + 5m + 6$
  c $m^2 + 5m + 6 = (m + 3)(m + 2)$
  d $f = m^2 + 5m + 6$
  e $m^2 + 5m + 6 = m(m + 5) + 6$

PS 2 Which of the following are not identities?

  A $1 - 2(a - 1) = -2a - 1$ **B** $1 - 2(a - 1) = -2a + 3$
  C $1 - 2(a - 1) = 1 - 2a - 2$ **D** $1 - 2(a - 1) = 1 - 2a + 2$
  E $1 - 2(a - 1) = 1 + 2a + 2$

PS 3 a Write down one value of x for which the statement $(x + 4)^2 = x^2 + 4^2$ is true.

  b Linda says that $(x + 4)^2 = x^2 + 4^2$ is true for all values of x.
   Is Linda correct? Explain your answer.

  c Which of these are identities?
   A $(x + 4)^2 \equiv x^2 + 4^2$ **B** $(x + 4)^2 \equiv x^2 + 4x + 16$ **C** $(x + 4)^2 \equiv x^2 + 8x + 16$
   D $(x + 4)^2 \equiv x^2 + 4x + 8$ **E** $(x + 4)^2 \equiv x^2 + 8x + 8$

DF / ES 4 Dave is three times older than Anne.
Julie is 5 years older than Anne.
Julie is twice as old as Colin.
Anne is x years old.

  a Write down an expression, in terms of x, for the sum of their ages.
  b Write down the integer values of x, for which
   i Dave is the oldest of the four
   ii Julie is the oldest of the four.

DF / ES 5 $x^2 - 4x - 9$ can be written in the form $(x - 2)^2 + k$.

  a Work out the value of k.
  b Solve the equation $x^2 - 4x - 9 = 0$.

Algebra Strand 1 Starting algebra Unit 11 Identities

6 Work out the values of a, b and c if
$(x + 5)^2 + (x - 4)^2 = ax^2 + bx + c$.

7 a Show that the area of this shape is $9y^2 + 2y - 24$.

  b Leo says the area is 24 cm².
  Explain why this is not true.

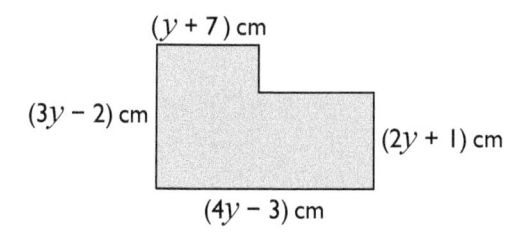

$(y + 7)$ cm
$(3y - 2)$ cm
$(2y + 1)$ cm
$(4y - 3)$ cm

8 Show that

  a $\dfrac{x+1}{3} - \dfrac{x-1}{2} = \dfrac{5-x}{6}$

  b $\dfrac{1}{1-x} + \dfrac{1}{1+x} = \dfrac{2}{1-x^2}$

9 Prove that

  a The sum of any two odd numbers is always even.

  b The sum of the squares of two consecutive numbers is always odd.

  c The difference between the squares of any two odd numbers is always even.

10 Explain why the area of this triangle can never be a whole number of cm² when x is an odd number.

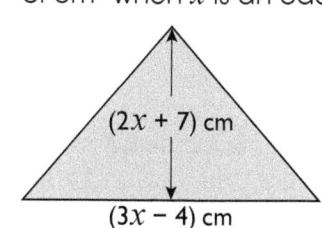

$(2x + 7)$ cm
$(3x - 4)$ cm

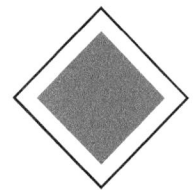

Algebra Strand 2 Sequences
Unit 5 Quadratic sequences

PS PRACTISING SKILLS **DF** DEVELOPING FLUENCY **PB** PROBLEM SOLVING **ES** EXAM-STYLE

PS ES 1
a Write down the first four terms of a quadratic sequence with nth term $2n^2 - 6n + 5$.

b Explain why every term of this sequence is an odd number.

PS ES 2 Here are the first few terms of a sequence.
0, 4, 18, 48, 100, …

a Explain why this is not a quadratic sequence.

b Find the 10th term.

DF ES 3 The nth term of an arithmetic sequence is $2n + 10$.
The nth term of a quadratic sequence is $n^2 - n$.

a Which number appears in both sequences and in the same position?

b Otis says that there are only three terms in the quadratic sequence that are not in the arithmetic sequence. Explain why Otis is correct and write down these three terms.

DF ES 4 Here is a pattern made from dots.

Pattern 1   Pattern 2   Pattern 3   Pattern 4   Pattern 5

a Copy the patterns. In each pattern, join each pair of dots with a straight line.

b Write down the number of lines in each pattern.

c The number of lines drawn in each pattern forms a quadratic sequence. Write down the nth term of this sequence.

PB ES 5 $n^2 + 4n$ is the nth term of a quadratic sequence.
$2n^2 - 5n$ is the nth term of a different quadratic sequence.

a Angus says that the number 12 appears in both sequences. Is Angus right? Explain your answer.

b For what value of n is the term the same in both sequences?

Algebra Strand 2 Sequences Unit 5 Quadratic sequences

6 In this pattern, lines are drawn from each vertex to the mid-point of each side inside some regular polygons.

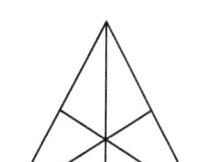

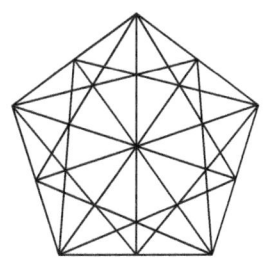

   a Write down the number of lines drawn inside each of these polygons.

   b How many lines would there be inside a regular hexagon?

   c i The number of lines in the pattern forms a quadratic sequence. Write down the nth term for this sequence.

   ii How many lines would there be in a 12-sided regular polygon?

7 Here are five of the first six terms of a quadratic sequence.

   2   4   7   ...   16   22

   a Write down the missing term.

   b What is the 20th term of this sequence?

   c Write down the position-to-term formula.

8 Here is a pattern made from black and white triangular tiles.

   a Write down an expression in terms of n for the sequence of black triangles.

   b Write down an expression in terms of n for the sequence of white triangles.

   c Show that the sequence formed by the total number of small triangles in each pattern is the sequence of square numbers.

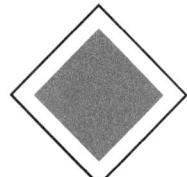

Algebra Strand 2 Sequences
Unit 6 Geometric progressions

PS — PRACTISING SKILLS **DF** — DEVELOPING FLUENCY **PB** — PROBLEM SOLVING **ES** — EXAM-STYLE

PS 1 These sequences are geometric progressions. Write down the common ratio for each one.

   a 100, 50, 25, 12.5, …

   b 4, 6, 9, 13.5, …

   c 243, 81, 27, 9, …

   d 8, 11.2, 15.68, 21.952, …

PS 2 Write down the first four terms of each geometric progression.

   a first term 1, common ratio 4

   b first term 8, common ratio 1.5

   c first term 64 000, common ratio 0.25

   d first term 1, common ratio 0.1

DF ES 3 Here are the first five terms of a geometric progression.

   10, 20, 40, 80, 160, …

   a i Write down the next term in the geometric progression.

   ii Explain how you got your answer to part **i**.

   b Show that the nth term of this geometric progression is $10 \times 2n$.

DF ES 4 The first term of a geometric progression is 1. The common ratio is 5.

   a Write down the first five terms of this geometric progression.

   b The odd-numbered terms of this geometric progression form a different sequence.

   i What is the common ratio of this geometric sequence?

   ii Write down the fifth term of the new sequence.

Algebra Strand 2 Sequences Unit 6 Geometric progressions

5 £25 000 is invested at an annual compound interest rate of 4%.
The values of this investment after each year form a geometric progression.

  a Work out how much the investment is worth after

  i 1 year

  ii 2 years

  iii 3 years

  iv 4 years.

  b The values form a geometric progression. What is the common ratio?

6 Roger buys a second-hand car for £12 000.
Its value depreciates by 10% each year.

  a Show that the values of the car each year form a geometric progression.

  b What is the common ratio of this geometric progression?

  c After how many years is the value of the car first less than £5000?

7 3 and 9 are the second and third terms of one geometric progression and the first and second terms of a different geometric progression.

  a Work out the difference between the fifth terms of the two geometric progressions.

  b Describe the geometric progression formed by the differences of corresponding terms.

8 In 2001, Tom and Bella each invested a sum of money in a different company.
Tom invested £25 000 in Company A.
Bella invested £5000 in Company B.
Tom's investment decreased by 12.5% each year.
Bella's investment increased by 15% each year.

  a Work out the values of Tom and Bella's investments (in pounds) each year for the first ten years of each investment.

  b In what year was Bella's investment first worth more than Tom's investment?

9 The first term of a sequence is 1 and the fifth term is 25.
Write down the first five terms of the sequence if it is a

  a linear sequence

  b quadratic sequence

  c geometric progression.

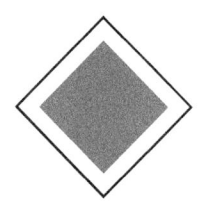

Algebra Strand 3 Functions and graphs Unit 5 Finding equations of straight lines

PS — PRACTISING SKILLS   **DF** — DEVELOPING FLUENCY   **PB** — PROBLEM SOLVING   **ES** — EXAM-STYLE

PS 1 Write down the equation of the line that has a gradient of
  a 6 and goes through (1, 5)
  b −4 and goes through (3, 10)
  c 3.5 and goes through (−2, −12).

PS 2 Triangle PQR is drawn on a co-ordinate grid.
  a Write down the equations of the three lines that make this triangle.
  b Work out the area of triangle PQR.

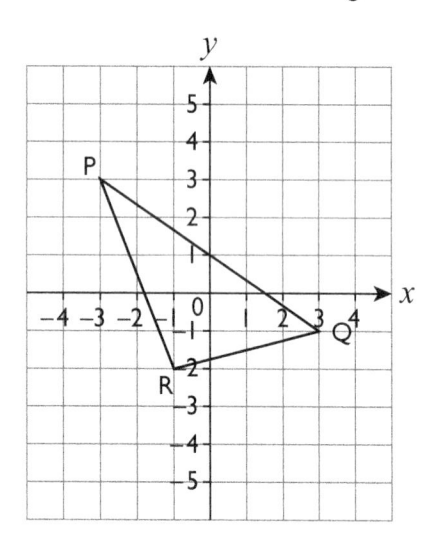

3 The graph shows the prices charged by Safe Car Hire.

It shows the relationship between the charge (£C) and the number of days (n) for which the car is hired.

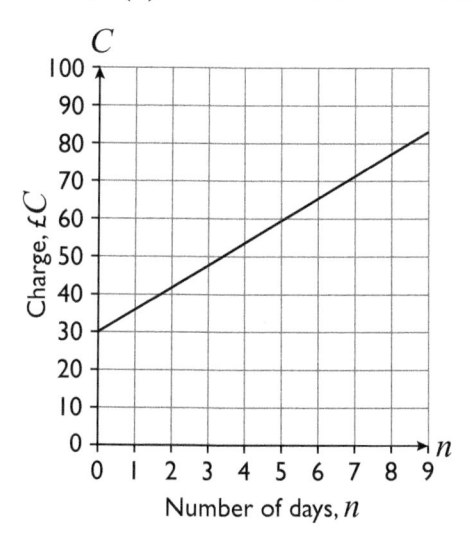

a i Write down the gradient of this graph.

  ii What does this gradient represent?

b Write down the equation of this straight-line graph.

c Alan hires a car from Safe Car Hire for 20 days. Work out the total charge.

4 The graph shows the time, T minutes, to cook a turkey with mass m lb.

T is given by the formula $T = am + b$.

a Work out the values of a and b.

b Work out the cooking time of a turkey with a mass of 26 lb.

Give your answer in hours and minutes.

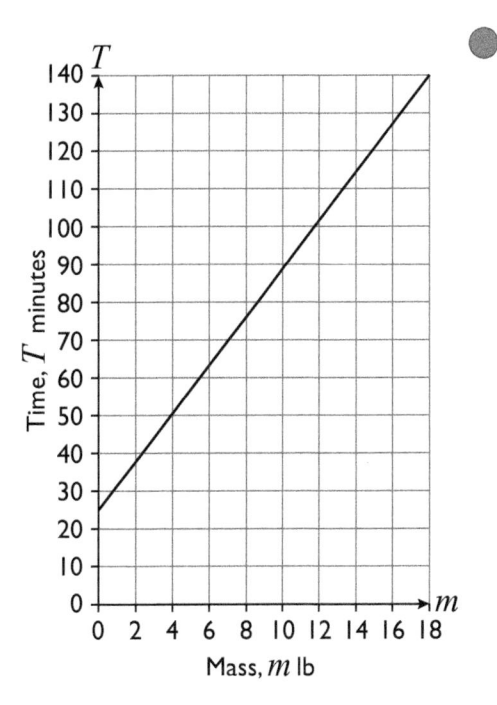

Algebra Strand 3 Functions and graphs Unit 5 Finding equations of straight lines

5 Line l goes through the points A(0, 5) and B(5, 0).
Line m goes through the points D(0, 2) and C(2, 0).
  a Write down the equation of each line.
  b Work out the area of the quadrilateral ABCD.

6 The two straight lines, p and q, are drawn on a co-ordinate grid.
  a Write down the equation of each line.
  b Write down the equation of the straight line that is parallel to p and passes through (1, 5).
  c What are the co-ordinates of the point where lines p and q intersect?

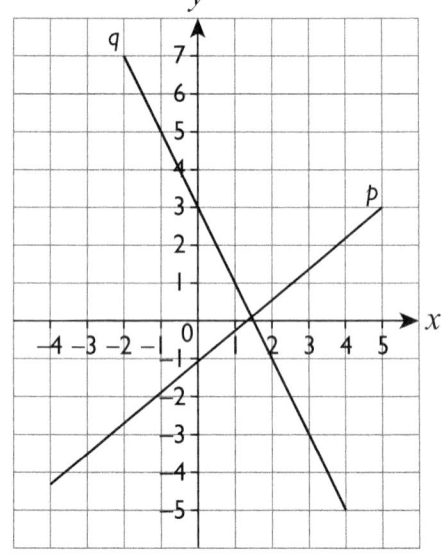

7 A square has vertices A(3, 3), B(3, −2), C(−2, −2) and D(−2, 3).
  a Write down the equations of the diagonals.
  b What is the product of the gradients of the two diagonals?

8 a Write down the gradient of the straight line that joins the points E(5, 8) and F(−3, 20).
  b Toby says that the straight line that goes through E and F will extend through the point G(40, −45).
   Is Toby right?

9 Line l passes through points A(7, 2) and B(4, 4).
Line m has equation $2x + 3y = 5$.
  a Prove that l and m are parallel.
  b Line n has gradient 1.5 and passes through the mid-point of AB. Write down the equation for n.

10 A quadrilateral has vertices A(4, 5), B(9, 2), C(1, −1) and D(−4, 2).
  a Prove that ABCD is a parallelogram.
  b Write down the equation of the line that passes through A and C.

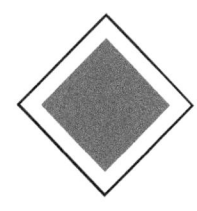

Algebra Strand 3 Functions and graphs Unit 6 Quadratic functions

PS — PRACTISING SKILLS   **DF** — DEVELOPING FLUENCY   **PB** — PROBLEM SOLVING   **ES** — EXAM-STYLE

PS ES 1 The graph shows the quadratic function $y = x^2 + x - 12$.

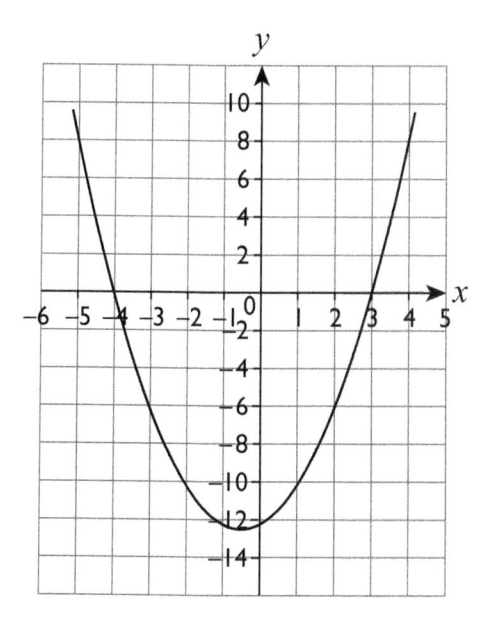

   a Write down the roots of $x^2 + x - 12 = 0$.

   b What are the approximate co-ordinates of the turning point?

   c Estimate the solutions of the equation $x^2 + x - 8 = 0$.

PS ES 2 A stone is dropped down a well.

   The distance of the stone from the top of the well in metres (d) is given by the formula $d = 5t^2$, where t is the number of seconds since the stone was dropped.

   a Draw a graph of d against t.

   b The well is 120 metres deep.

   How long will it take for the stone to reach the bottom of the well?

Algebra Strand 3 Functions and graphs Unit 6 Quadratic functions

PS **3** Alex throws a ball.
ES The table shows the height, d metres, of the ball after t seconds.

t	0	0.5	1.0	1.5	2.0	2.5	3.0	3.5
d	0	15	24	28	28	24	15	0

  a Draw a graph to show the path of the ball.
  b i Estimate the maximum height reached by the ball.
    ii What can you say about the velocity of the ball at its maximum height?

DF **4** The graph shows the quadratic function $y = x^2$.

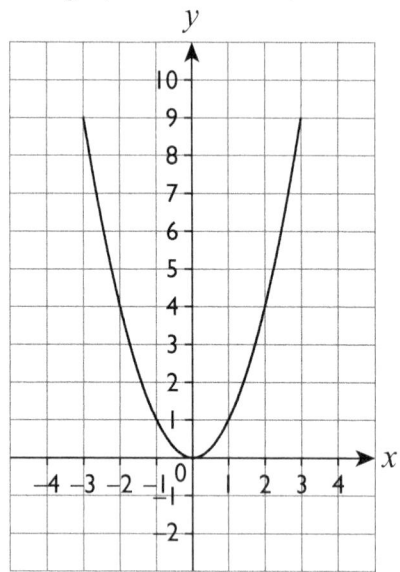

Use this graph to estimate solutions of each equation.
  a $x^2 = 4$
  b $x^2 = 6$
  c $x^2 - 2 = 0$
  d $x^2 + 3 = 0$
  e $x^2 = x + 2$

PS **5** A quadratic function has the equation $y = 2x^2 + x - 8$.
ES   **a** Copy and complete the table of values for the function.

x	-3	-2	-1	0	1	2	3
y	7		-7		-5		

  b Draw the graph of $y = 2x^2 + x - 8$.
  c Use your graph to solve the equation $2x^2 + x - 8 = 0$.

Algebra Strand 3 Functions and graphs Unit 6 Quadratic functions

6 a Sketch a graph of $y = (x - 2)(x + 5)$ showing clearly where the graph crosses the axes.
  b Write down the equation of the line of symmetry.
  c Write down the approximate co-ordinates of the turning point.

7 a Draw the graph of the quadratic function with roots $x = -1$ and $x = 3$ and a turning point of $(1, -4)$.
  b Write down the equation of a quadratic function that has roots $x = -1$ and $x = 3$ and a turning point of $(1, 4)$.

8 Here are five graphs.

a

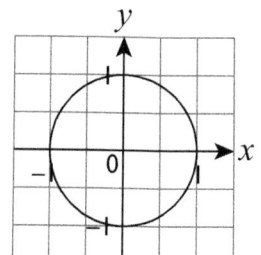

b

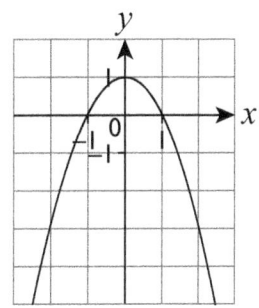

c

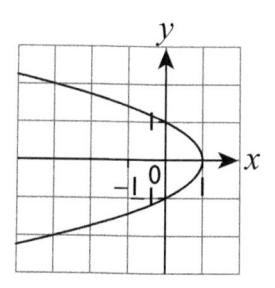

d

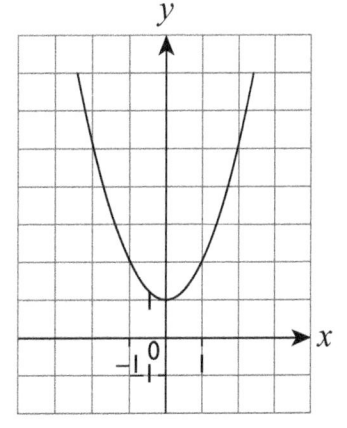

e

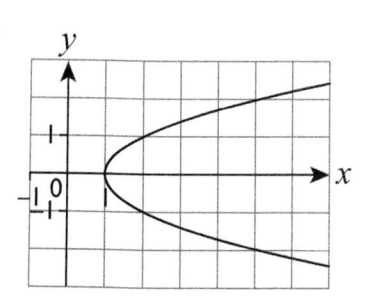

Their equations are

  i $y = x^2 + 1$
  ii $x = y^2 + 1$
  iii $y = 1 - x^2$
  iv $x = 1 - y^2$
  v $y^2 + x^2 = 1$

Match each graph with the correct equation.

45

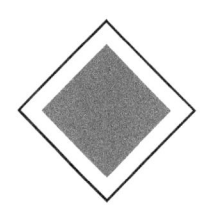

Algebra Strand 3 Functions and graphs Unit 7 Polynomial and reciprocal functions

PS PRACTISING SKILLS **DF** DEVELOPING FLUENCY **PB** PROBLEM SOLVING **ES** EXAM-STYLE

PS **ES** **1** A curve has the equation $y = x^3 - 2x^2 - 4x$.

    a Copy and complete the table of values for the function.

x	−2	−1	0	1	2	3	4
y	−8		0			−3	

    b Draw the graph of $y = x^3 - 2x^2 - 4x$.

    c Use your graph to estimate solutions of the equation $x^3 - 2x^2 - 4x = -5$.

PB **ES** **2** The volume V of this cuboid is given by the formula $V = x(x - 2)(x - 4)$.

    a **i** Copy and complete this table for $V = x(x - 2)(x - 4)$

x	0	1	2	3	4	5
V	0		0			15

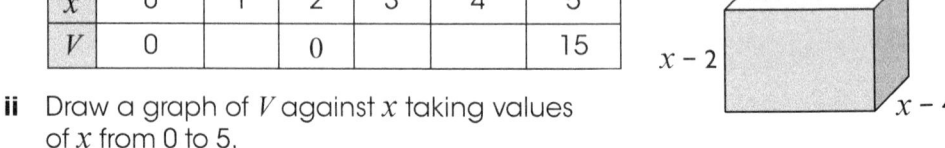

        ii Draw a graph of V against x taking values of x from 0 to 5.

    b Use your graph to estimate the dimensions of the cuboid when $V = 2$. Explain why only one value of x is acceptable.

PS **ES** **3 a** Copy and complete this table for $y = x + \dfrac{1}{x}$.

x	−8	−4	−2	−0.5	−0.25	0	0.25	0.5	2	4	8
y	−8.125				−4.25				2.5		

    b Sketch a graph of $y = x + \dfrac{1}{x}$.

Algebra Strand 4 Algebraic methods Unit 2 Linear inequalities

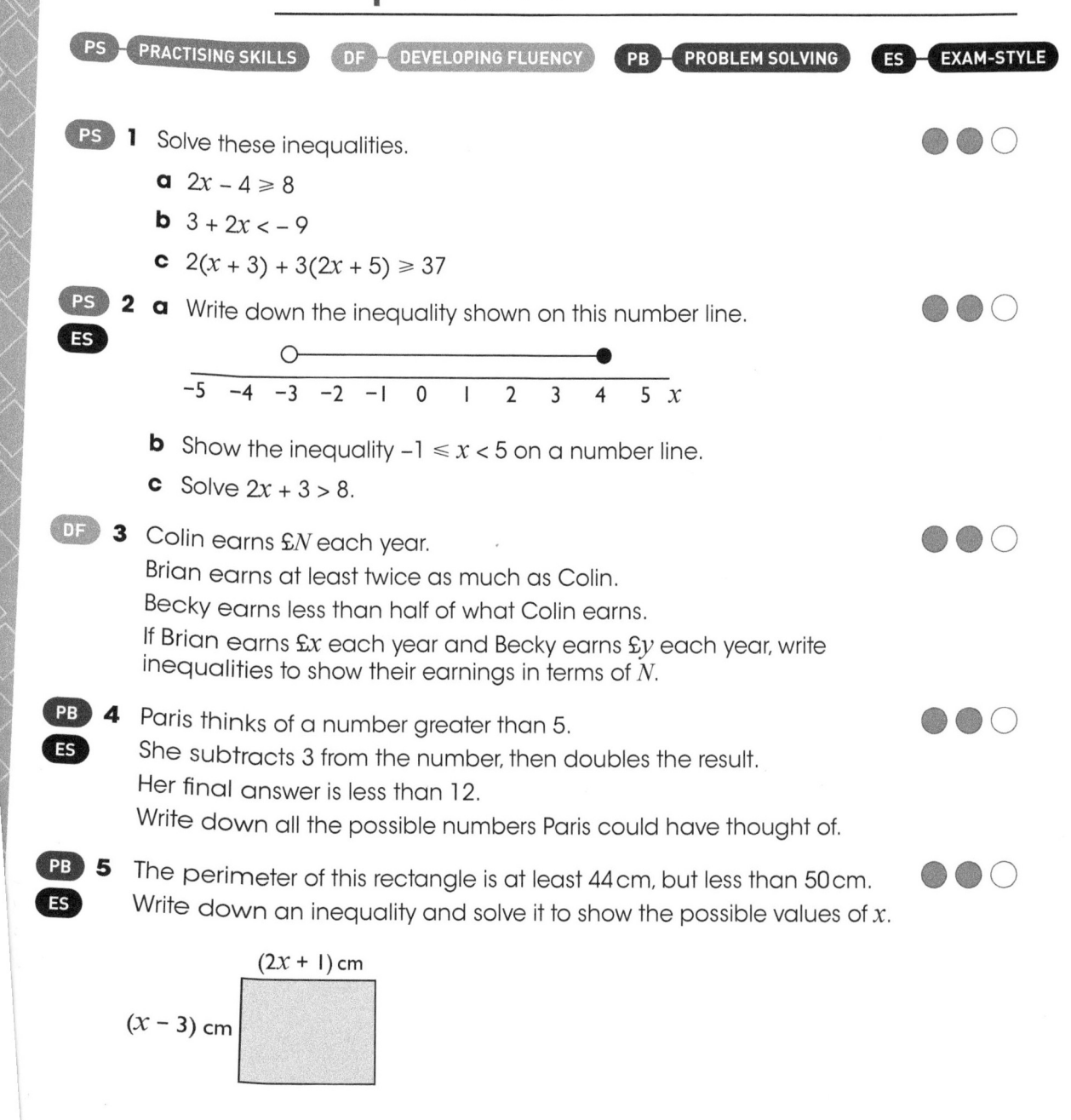

PS PRACTISING SKILLS **DF** DEVELOPING FLUENCY **PB** PROBLEM SOLVING **ES** EXAM-STYLE

PS 1 Solve these inequalities.
  a $2x - 4 \geq 8$
  b $3 + 2x < -9$
  c $2(x + 3) + 3(2x + 5) \geq 37$

PS ES 2 a Write down the inequality shown on this number line.

$-5\ -4\ -3\ -2\ -1\ 0\ 1\ 2\ 3\ 4\ 5\ x$

  b Show the inequality $-1 \leq x < 5$ on a number line.
  c Solve $2x + 3 > 8$.

DF 3 Colin earns £N each year.
Brian earns at least twice as much as Colin.
Becky earns less than half of what Colin earns.
If Brian earns £x each year and Becky earns £y each year, write inequalities to show their earnings in terms of N.

PB ES 4 Paris thinks of a number greater than 5.
She subtracts 3 from the number, then doubles the result.
Her final answer is less than 12.
Write down all the possible numbers Paris could have thought of.

PB ES 5 The perimeter of this rectangle is at least 44 cm, but less than 50 cm.
Write down an inequality and solve it to show the possible values of x.

$(2x + 1)$ cm
$(x - 3)$ cm

Algebra Strand 3 Functions and graphs Unit 7 Polynomial and reciprocal functions

4 a Copy and complete this table for the curve $y = x^3 - 4x$

x	-3	-2	-1	0	1	2	3
y		0			-3		

  b Draw the graph of $y = x^3 - 4x$ for x from -3 to 3.

5 Sketch graphs of the following equations.
  For each sketch, write down the co-ordinates of any x- or y-intercepts.

  a $y = x^3$
  b $y = \dfrac{1}{x}$
  c $y = x^3 + 1$

6 a Copy and complete the table of values for $y = x^2 + 2x - 2$.

x	-3	-2	-1	0	1	2	3
y			-3			6	

  b Draw the graph of $y = x^2 + 2x - 2$.
  c Write down the co-ordinates of the turning point.
  d Use the graph to solve $x^2 + 2x - 2 = 0$.

7 a On the same pair of axes, draw the graphs of $y = x^2 - x$ and $y = 2 - \dfrac{1}{x}$.
  b Show that the points of intersection of these two graphs are solutions of the equation $x^3 - x^2 - 2x + 1 = 0$.
  c What is the approximate positive value of each solution?

6 April, Bavinda and Chas each have some marbles.
April has 15 more marbles than Bavinda.
Bavinda has three times as many marbles as Chas.
Together they have less than 200 marbles.
What is the greatest number of marbles that April can have?

7 Write down an inequality for each of the following.

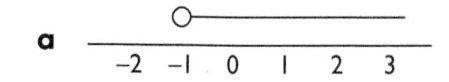

a number line from -2 to 3 with open circle at 1 extending right

b number line from -2 to 3 with closed circle at 2 extending left

c number line from -2 to 3 with closed circles at -1 and 2

d number line from -2 to 3 with closed circle at -1 and open circle at 2

8 Solve
   a $5x + 3 > 20$
   b $2(3x - 1) \leq 34$

9 Show these inequalities on a number line.
   a $x < 3$
   b $x \geq -2$
   c $-2 \leq 3x + 1 \leq 7$
   d $-1 < 1 - x < 5$

10 n is an integer that satisfies the inequality $5n - 1 > 4n + 2$.
Which one of these inequalities can n not satisfy?
$4n + 5 > n + 2$ $2n - 7 > 1 - n$ $n + 4 > 6n - 8$ $7 - n > 2n - 11$

11 n is an integer that satisfies both of these inequalities:
$4n - 1 < 2n + 3$ and $5(n + 4) \geq 2(n + 5)$
Write down all the possible values of n.

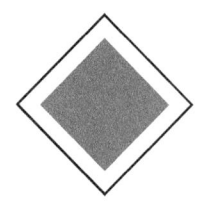

Algebra Strand 4 Algebraic methods Unit 3 Solving pairs of equations by substitution

PS PRACTISING SKILLS **DF** DEVELOPING FLUENCY **PB** PROBLEM SOLVING **ES** EXAM-STYLE

PS 1 Solve these pairs of simultaneous equations by substitution.
  a $2x + y = 6$
   $y = x + 3$
  b $x + 4y = 11$
   $x = y + 1$
  c $2x + 3y = 6$
   $x = 5 - 2y$

PS 2 Solve these pairs of simultaneous equations by substitution.
  a $y = 5x - 1$
   $3x + 2y = 24$
  b $x + 4y = 11$
   $y = 2x + 5$

DF ES 3 Dale thinks of two numbers.
The difference between the two numbers is 7.
The sum of the two numbers is 25.
What two numbers is Dale thinking of?

DF ES 4 The sum of two numbers is 160.
The difference between the two numbers is 102.
Work out the two numbers.

DF ES 5 Ben pays £10.50 for 4 portions of fish and 3 portions of chips
Tracey pays £5.40 for 3 portions of fish.
Malcolm buys 2 portions of fish and 2 portions of chips.
How much should this cost him?

DF ES 6 Chan has exactly 24 notes in his wallet.
They are either £20 notes or £10 notes.
The total value of the notes is £410.
How many £20 notes are in Chan's wallet?

50

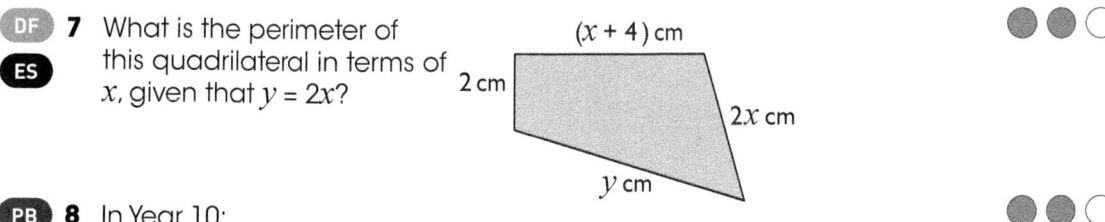

7 What is the perimeter of this quadrilateral in terms of x, given that $y = 2x$?

$(x + 4)$ cm, 2 cm, $2x$ cm, y cm

8 In Year 10:
- There are b boys and g girls.
- There are 45 more boys than girls.

If 12 boys and no girls joined Year 10, there would be twice as many boys as there are girls.

How many students are in Year 10?

9 A tennis club has f female members and m male members.

In 2010, they had 16 more female members than male members.

By 2015, the number of female members had increased by one-third, the number of male members had decreased by 18 and there were a total of 120 members.

How many female members did the club have in 2010?

10 An equation of line l is given by $y = mx + c$.

The points $(1, 7)$ and $(3, 11)$ lie on line l.

Work out the values of m and c.

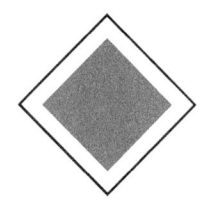

Algebra Strand 4 Algebraic methods Unit 4 Solving simultaneous equations by elimination

PS — PRACTISING SKILLS   **DF** — DEVELOPING FLUENCY   **PB** — PROBLEM SOLVING   **ES** — EXAM-STYLE

PS 1 Solve these pairs of simultaneous equations by elimination.

  a $3x + 2y = 14$
     $5x - 2y = 18$

  b $2x + 3y = 2$
     $8x + 3y = 17$

  c $6x - 5y = 23$
     $4x - 3y = 14$

PB ES 2 The prices of tickets for a football match are £a for adults and £c for children.
Barry pays £270 for tickets for 2 adults and 5 children.
Jim pays £251 for tickets for 3 adults and 2 children.
Peter has £150 to buy tickets for the football match. Does he have enough money to buy tickets for himself and his 3 children?

PB ES 3 A taxi company charges a fixed amount plus an additional cost per mile.
A journey of 8 miles costs £8.90. A journey of 12 miles costs £12.10.
Susan is 20 miles from home. She has only £20.
Does Susan have enough money to travel home by taxi?

PB ES 4 Work out the area of this rectangle.

Top: $(5x + 5y)$ cm
Left: $(6y - 5)$ cm
Right: $(5x + 9)$ cm
Bottom: $(2x + 3)$ cm

5 The Smith family and the Jones family have booked the same summer holiday.

Mr and Mrs Smith and their three children paid £2440.

Mr Jones, his mother and father and his son paid £2330.

After they book, the travel company reduces the cost of a child's holiday by 10% and refunds both families.

How much refund should each family receive?

6 The diagram shows an equilateral triangle and a square.

The perimeter of the square is equal to the perimeter of the triangle.

Work out the area of the square.

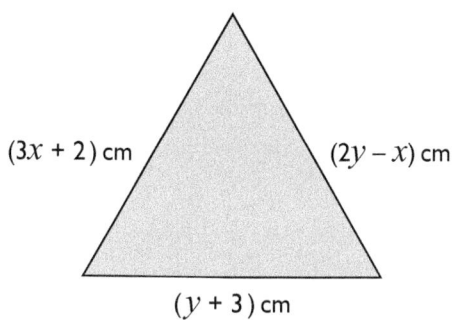

$(3x + 2)$ cm $(2y - x)$ cm

$(y + 3)$ cm

7 A boy travels for x hours at a speed of 5 km/h.

He then travels for y hours at a speed of 10 km/h.

In total, he travels 35 km at an average speed of 7 km/h.

Work out the values of x and y.

8 In one week, Liz works 35 hours at her standard rate of pay and 12 hours at her overtime rate. For this, she is paid £428.40.

In a different week, Liz works 40 hours at her standard rate of pay and 8 hours at her overtime rate. For this, she is paid £425.60.

a Work out Liz's standard rate of pay.

b Work out the ratio of the standard rate of pay to the overtime rate of pay.

9 Two people bought identical Christmas decorations from the same shop.

One paid £65.60 for 200 streamers and 220 tree decorations.

The other paid £63.30 for 210 streamers and 200 tree decorations.

How much would it cost to buy 200 streamers and 200 tree decorations from this shop?

10 The points (2, 2.5) and (6, −2.5) lie on the line with equation $ax + by = c$.

a Bob says the point (−2, 8) also lies on this line.

Is Bob correct?

b Write down

i the gradient of this line

ii the co-ordinates of the intercepts on the axes.

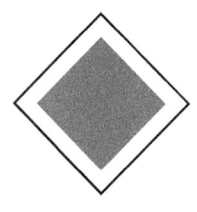

Algebra Strand 4 Algebraic methods Unit 5 Using graphs to solve simultaneous equations

PS PRACTISING SKILLS **DF** DEVELOPING FLUENCY **PB** PROBLEM SOLVING **ES** EXAM-STYLE

PS **1** **a** Draw the graphs of $y = 2x + 3$ and $y = 3 - x$ on the same pair of axes.

b Write down the co-ordinates of the point where the two lines intersect.

c Check your answer to part **b** by solving the two equations using algebra.

PS **2** **a** Draw the graphs of $2x + y = 3$ and $x - 2y = 4$ on the same pair of axes.

b Write down the co-ordinates of the point where the two lines intersect.

c Use algebra to check your answer to part **b**.

d Work out the area of the region bounded by the lines $2x + y = 3$ and $x - 2y = 4$ and the y-axis.

DF **ES** **3** Taxi companies charge a fixed amount plus an additional cost per mile.

Toni's taxis	Colin's cabs
£2.50 plus £1.20 per mile.	£5.00 plus 75p per mile.

a On the same pair of axes, draw graphs to show the cost, £C, of a journey of x miles for each taxi company.

b What useful information does the point of intersection of the two graphs give you?

c Harry wants to travel 7 miles by taxi. Which company would you recommend?

DF **ES** **4** By drawing graphs, find the approximate solutions of
$15x + 8y = 60$
$4x - 9y = 54$

Algebra Strand 4 Algebraic methods Unit 5 Using graphs to solve simultaneous equations

DF 5 Line l has equation $x + y = 5$.
Line m has equation $y = 3x + 3$.
Line n has equation $y = x + 1$.
By looking at the graph, solve each pair of simultaneous equations.

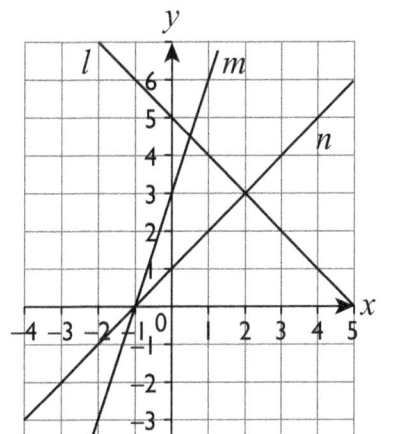

a $x + y = 5$
$y = x + 1$

b $y = 3x + 3$
$y = x + 1$

c $x + y = 5$
$y = 3x + 3$

DF ES 6 Two cars are travelling towards each other along a straight road.
The distance, d metres, from O after t seconds is given for each car by
Car A $\quad d = 10 + 30t \quad$ Car B $\quad d = 120 - 20t$

a On the same axes, draw graphs to show this information.

b Use your graph to help answer these questions.
   i At what time were both cars the same distance from O?
   ii How far from O were the cars at this time?

DF ES 7 The graph shows the speed, v metres per second, of a car after t seconds.

a Write down the equation of this graph in the form $v = u + at$, where u and a are constants.

b The speed of a second car is given by the equation $v = 80 - 2.5t$. Draw this line on a copy of the graph.

c i After how many seconds are the two cars travelling at the same speed?
  ii Estimate this speed.

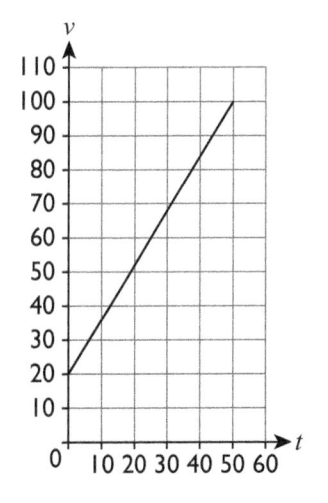

DF 8 a Write down the equation of the straight line that passes through
   i A and C
   ii D and B.

b Write down the co-ordinates of the point of intersection of the two equations in part **a**.

c Use algebra to check your answer to part **b**.

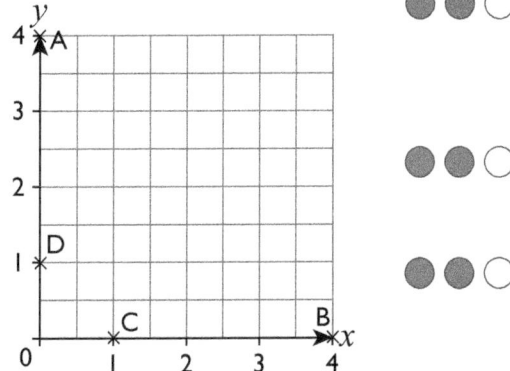

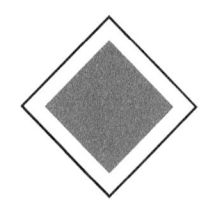

Algebra Strand 5 Working with quadratics Unit 1 Factorising quadratics

PS PRACTISING SKILLS   **DF** DEVELOPING FLUENCY   **PB** PROBLEM SOLVING   **ES** EXAM-STYLE

PS 1 Factorise each expression.
  a $x^2 + 2x$
  b $x^2 - 81$
  c $x^2 - 8x + 4x - 32$
  d $x^2 - 9x + 14$
  e $x^2 + 3x - 40$
  f $x^2 - 9$

PB ES 2 Amir and Winona factorised $x^2 + 5x - 6$.
Amir wrote $x^2 + 5x - 6 = (x + 2)(x + 3)$.
Winona wrote $x^2 + 5x - 6 = (x + 2)(x - 3)$.
Explain why each answer is wrong and give the correct answer.

PB ES 3 The area of a square is given by the expression $x^2 - 6x + 9$.
Write an expression for the side length of the square.

PB ES 4 The diagram shows three rectangles.

Rectangle A: $x + 1$ by $x + 2$
Rectangle B: $x - 1$ by $x + 4$
Rectangle C: x by $x + 7$

The area of a fourth rectangle D can be found using the equation:
Area D = Area A – Area B + Area C.
What are the dimensions of rectangle D?

PB 5 Work out each of these. Do not use a calculator.
  a $101^2 - 99^2$
  b $63^2 + 2 \times 63 \times 37 + 37^2$
  c $9^4 - 1^4$

56

Algebra Strand 5 Working with quadratics Unit 1 Factorising quadratics

6 Sandy thinks of any number, n.
She squares her number, subtracts two times her original number from the result and then subtracts 48.
Write down a fully factorised expression in n for her final result.

7 The volume of the cuboid shown is $a^3 - 11a^2 + 30a$.

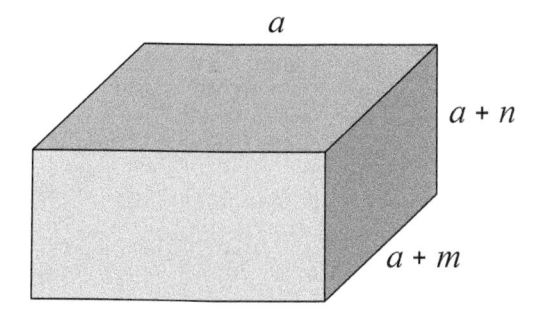

Work out the values of m and n, if $m > n$.

8 Without using a calculator, work out the area of the shaded part of this shape.

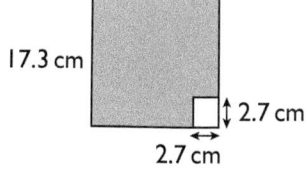

9 In this cuboid
the area of the front face is given by $p^2 + 17p + 70$
the area of the top face is given by $p^2 + 11p + 28$.

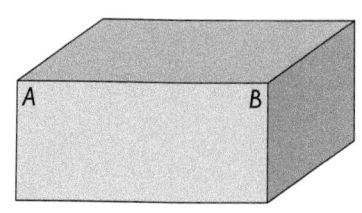

Write down an expression, in terms of p, for the length of the edge AB.

10 Fully simplify this expression.
$$\frac{x^2 + 5x - 24}{x^2 - 9x - 18}$$

57

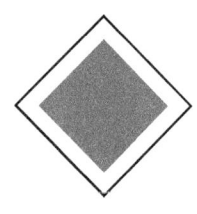

Algebra Strand 5 Working with quadratics Unit 2 Solving equations by factorising

PS PRACTISING SKILLS   **DF** DEVELOPING FLUENCY   **PB** PROBLEM SOLVING   **ES** EXAM-STYLE

PS 1 Solve these equations.
  a $(x + 1)(x + 2) = 0$
  b $(x - 4)(x - 5) = 0$
  c $x^2 + 9x = 0$
  d $x^2 - 2x - 24 = 0$
  e $x^2 = 36 - 5x$

PS 2 a The solutions of a quadratic equation are $x = 5$ and $x = -3$.
  Write down the quadratic equation.
  b The solutions of a quadratic equation are $y = -12$ and $y = -7$.
  Write down the quadratic equation.

DF ES 3 Here is Mnambi's attempt at solving $x^2 - x - 20 = 0$.
  $x^2 - x - 20 = 0$
  $(x - 5)(x + 4) = 0$
  $x = -5$ and $x = 4$
  Explain the mistakes that Mnambi made and give the correct solutions.

DF ES 4 Ed thinks of a number between 1 and 10.
  He squares the number and then subtracts his original number from the result.
  His final answer is 42.
  What was Ed's original number?

PB ES 5 A rectangle measures $(x + 1)$ cm by $(x + 2)$ cm.
  The area of the rectangle is 72 cm².
  What are the dimensions of the rectangle?

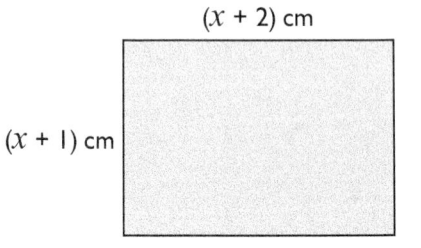

Algebra Strand 5 Working with quadratics Unit 2 Solving equations by factorising

PB ES 6 The diagram shows a rectangle and two trapeziums drawn inside a square of side length 20 cm.

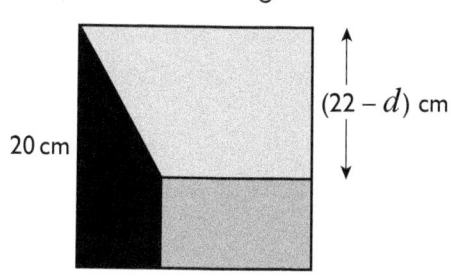

The area of the rectangle is 32 cm² and is given by $(d^2 - 4)$ cm².
Work out the area of each of the trapeziums.

PB ES 7 This shape is made from two identical right-angled triangles.
The total area of the shape is 135 cm².
Work out the length of the shortest side of one of these triangles.

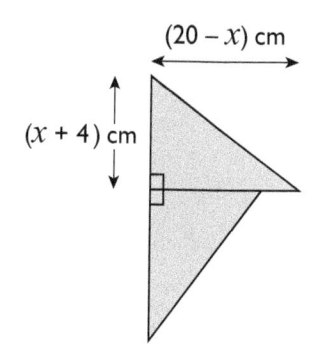

PB ES 8 The cuboid in the diagram has a total surface area of 246 cm².
Work out the volume of the cuboid.

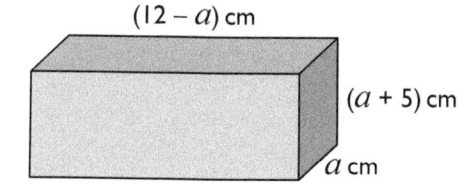

PB ES 9 What is the area of this right-angled triangle?

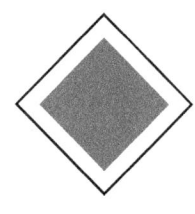

Geometry Strand 1 Units and scales Unit 11 Working with compound units

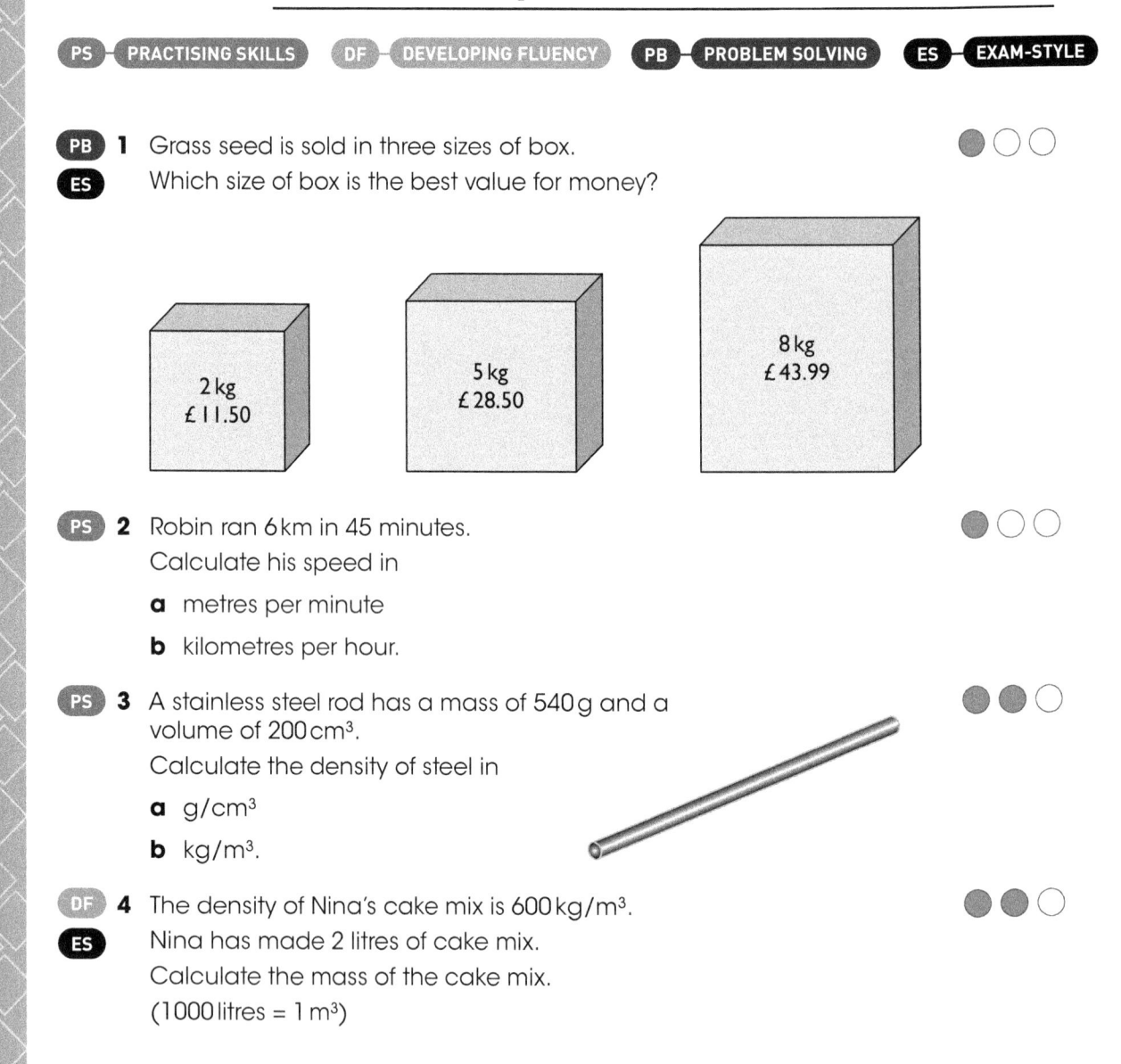

PS PRACTISING SKILLS **DF** DEVELOPING FLUENCY **PB** PROBLEM SOLVING **ES** EXAM-STYLE

PB
ES
1 Grass seed is sold in three sizes of box.
Which size of box is the best value for money?

2 kg £11.50

5 kg £28.50

8 kg £43.99

PS **2** Robin ran 6 km in 45 minutes.
Calculate his speed in
  a metres per minute
  b kilometres per hour.

PS **3** A stainless steel rod has a mass of 540 g and a volume of 200 cm³.
Calculate the density of steel in
  a g/cm³
  b kg/m³.

DF
ES
4 The density of Nina's cake mix is 600 kg/m³.
Nina has made 2 litres of cake mix.
Calculate the mass of the cake mix.
(1000 litres = 1 m³)

Geometry Strand 1 Units and scales Unit 11 Working with compound units

5 The plank of wood shown in the diagram has a mass of 7.5 kg.
Calculate its density in kg/m³.

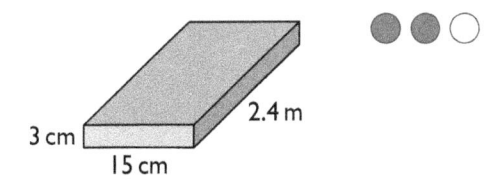

2.4 m
3 cm
15 cm

6 A steel girder weighs 2 tonnes.
The density of steel is 2500 kg/m³.
Calculate the volume of steel in the girder.
(1 tonne = 1000 kg)

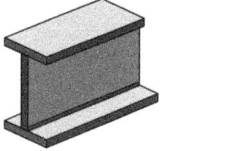

7 The graph shows Myra's car journey from her home to her mother's house.
Work out the average speed of this journey.

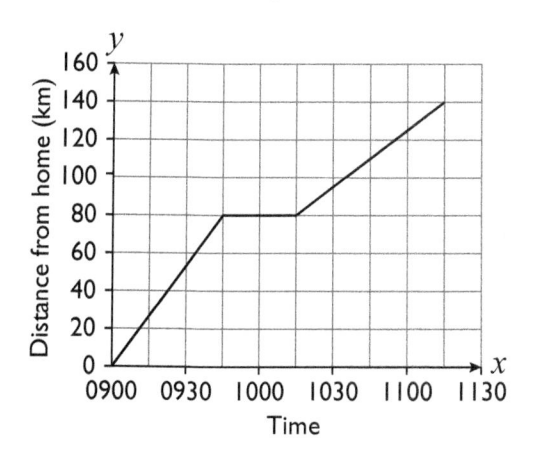

8 The ingot of gold shown in the diagram has a mass of 608 g.

  a Calculate the density of the gold.

  b What is the mass of a gold cube with side 10 cm?

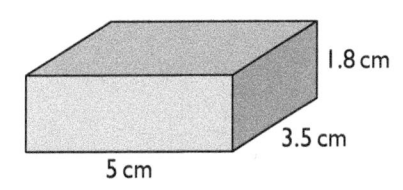

1.8 cm
3.5 cm
5 cm

61

9 This graph shows the cost of buying units of gas from ProGas each month.

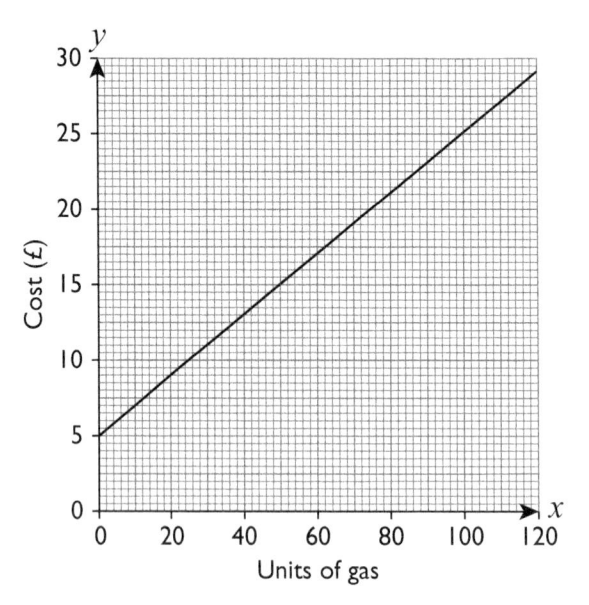

a What is the gradient of the straight line graph?

ProGas supply Daphne with her gas.

b Explain the cost of the gas that Daphne uses.

Daphne used 45 more units of gas in October than she did in September.

c The gas she used in October cost more than the gas she used in September. How much more?

10 At an oil refinery, oil is stored in tanks like the one shown.

The diameter of the tank is 20 m.
The depth of the oil in the tank is 5 m.
The density of the oil is 800 kg/m³.
An oil tanker can hold up to 50 000 kg of oil.
How many of these oil tankers are needed to empty all the oil from the tank?
Show all your working.

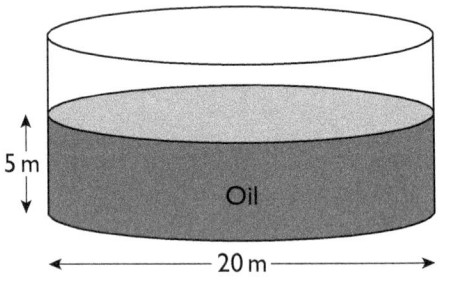

11 The bronze used to make bells is an alloy of copper and tin in the ratio 4 : 1 by mass.

The density of copper is 8.96 g/cm³.
The density of tin is 7.365 g/cm³.

a A bell has a mass of 2 tonnes. Work out
  i the mass of copper
  ii the mass of tin.

b Calculate the density of the bronze.

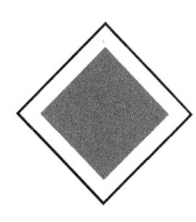

Geometry Strand 2
Properties of shapes Unit 9
Congruent triangles and proof

PS PRACTISING SKILLS   **DF** DEVELOPING FLUENCY   **PB** PROBLEM SOLVING   **ES** EXAM-STYLE

DF 1 State whether the triangles in each pair are congruent.
If they are, give a reason.

a 5 cm, 6 cm, 5 cm / 6 cm, 5 cm, 5 cm

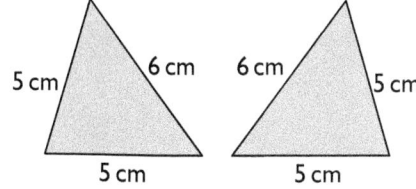

b 5 cm, 6 cm, 5 cm / 5 cm, 5 cm, 6 cm

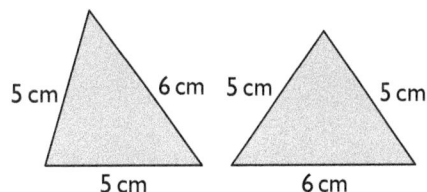

c 8 cm, 65°, 7.5 cm / 8 cm, 65°, 7.5 cm

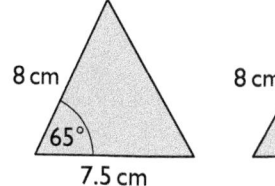

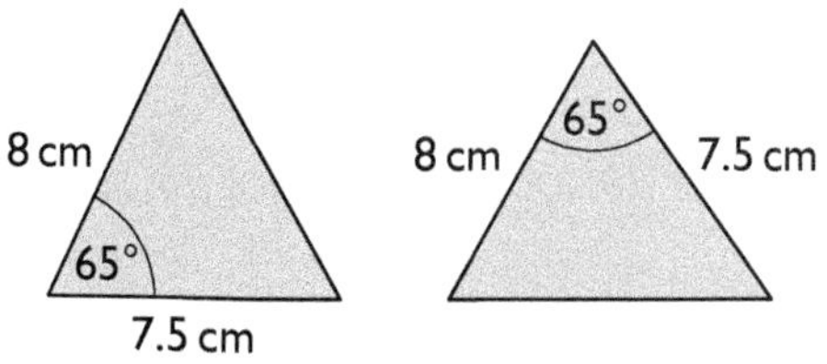

d 12 cm, 9 cm, 45° / 9 cm, 12 cm, 45°

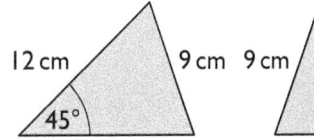

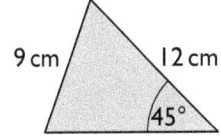

e 15 cm, 5 cm, right angle / 15 cm, 5 cm, right angle

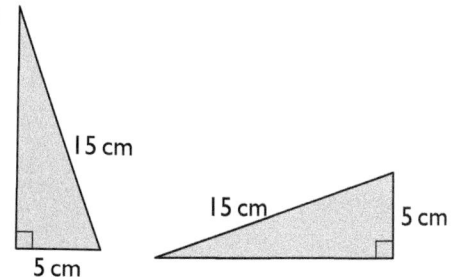

f 70°, 55° / 70°, 55°

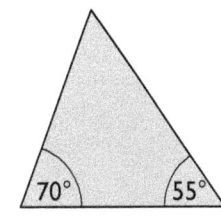

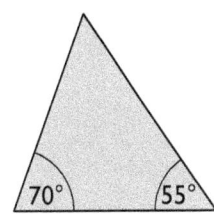

g 75°, 54°, 5 cm / 5 cm, 54°, 75°

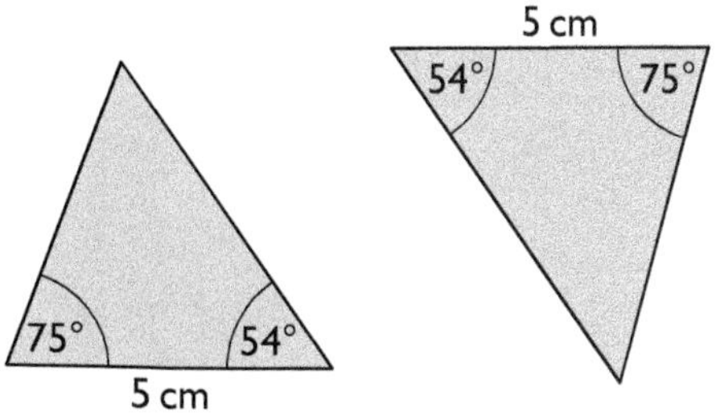

h 48°, 80°, 8 cm / 80°, 48°, 8 cm

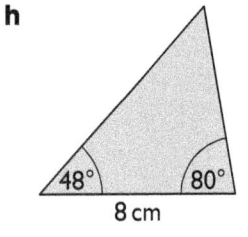

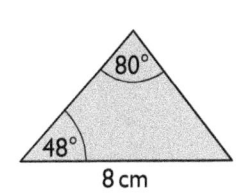

Geometry Strand 2 Properties of shapes Unit 9 Congruent triangles and proof

DF **2** The diagram shows a parallelogram, PQRS.
ES Prove that triangle PRS and triangle PQR are congruent.

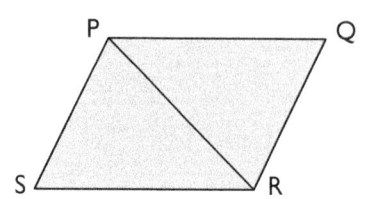

DF **3** Explain why triangles PQR and XYZ are not congruent.
ES

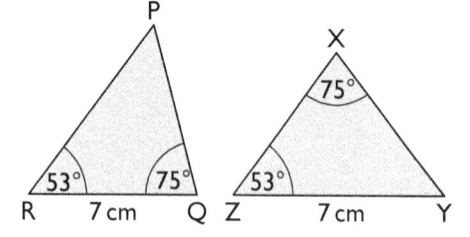

DF **4** ABCDEF is a regular hexagon.
ES Prove that BF = BD.

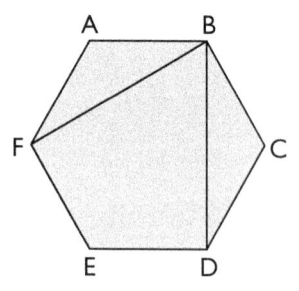

PS **5** PQR is an isosceles triangle with PQ = PR.
ES PS bisects the angle at P and the side RQ.
Prove that triangles PQS and PSR are congruent.

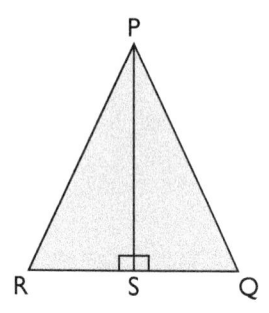

64

Geometry Strand 2 Properties of shapes Unit 9 Congruent triangles and proof

DF **6** ABCDE is a regular pentagon.
ES BFGC is a rectangle.
Prove that triangles ABF and DCG are congruent.

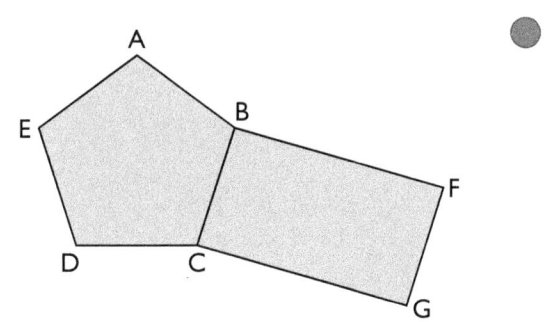

PB **7** In this diagram
ES AD = CD
$\angle A = \angle C = 90°$
Prove that DB bisects $\angle ABC$.

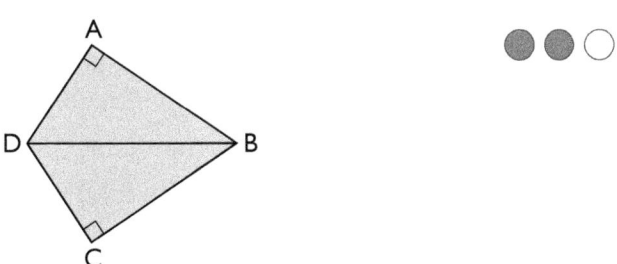

PB **8** In triangle EAD
ES EA = ED
$\angle AEB = \angle CED$.
Explain why AB = CD.

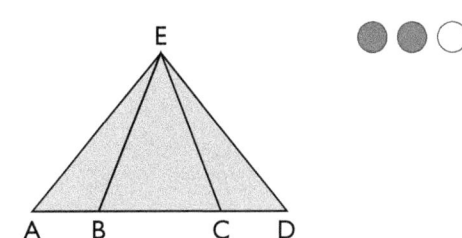

PB **9** ABCE is an isosceles trapezium.
ES BC = BD
AB is parallel to EDC.
ABDE is a parallelogram
Prove that triangles ABD and ADE are congruent.
Write down any assumptions you have made.

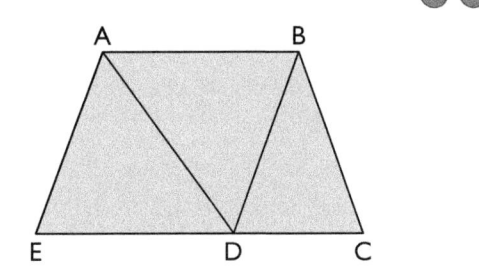

PB **10** ABC is a right-angled triangle.
ES ABED and ACFG are squares.
Prove that triangles ABG and ACD are congruent.

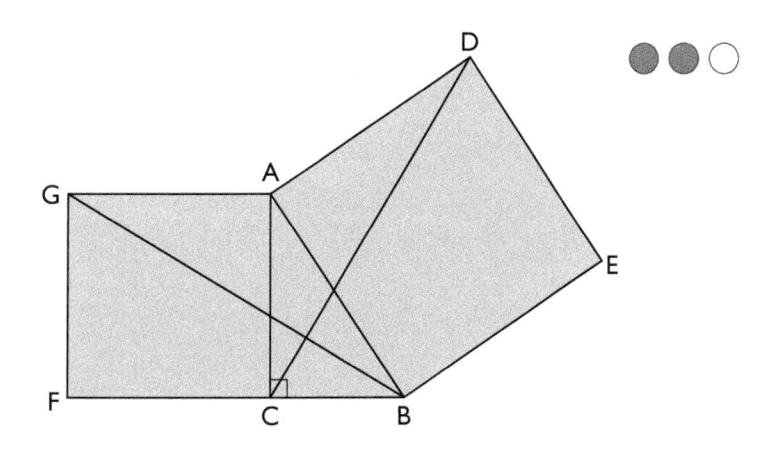

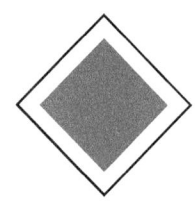

Geometry Strand 2
Properties of shapes
Unit 10 Proof using similar and congruent triangles

PS PRACTISING SKILLS **DF** DEVELOPING FLUENCY **PB** PROBLEM SOLVING **ES** EXAM-STYLE

PS **1** Show that triangle DEF is similar to triangle GHJ.
ES

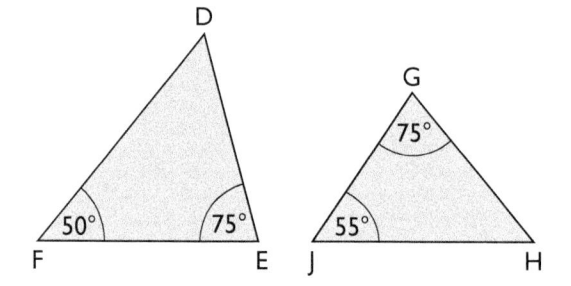

PS **2** PQRS, WXY and DEFG are parallel lines.
ES RX = XE
Prove that triangles QRX and EFX are congruent.

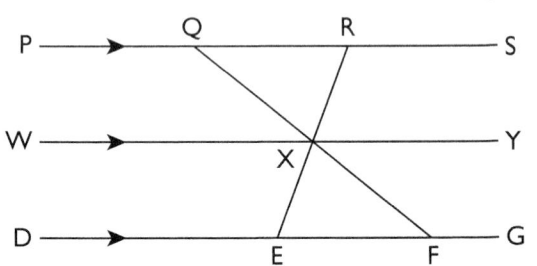

DF **3** AB is parallel to PQ.
Prove that triangles ABX and PQX are similar.

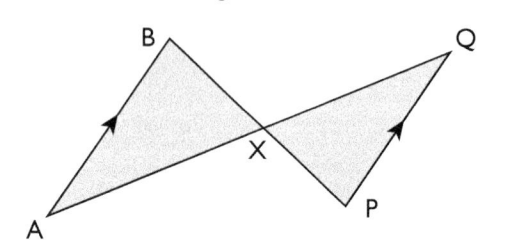

Geometry Strand 2 Properties of shapes Unit 10 Proof using similar and congruent triangles

DF 4 ABD and ACE are straight lines.
BC is parallel to DE.
Prove that triangles ABC and ADE are similar.

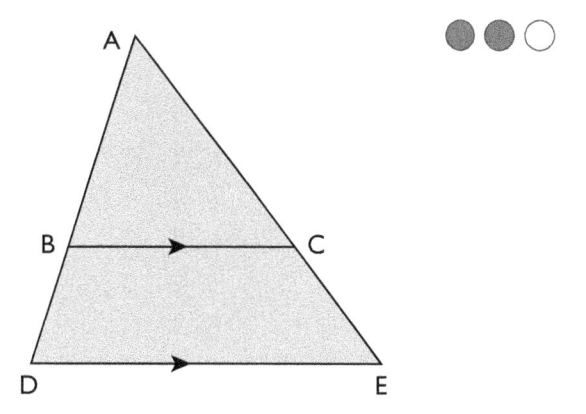

DF 5 For each part, state whether the two triangles are similar or congruent. Give a reason for each answer.

a

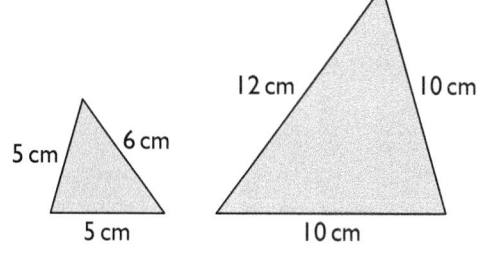

b

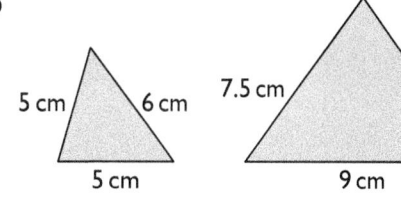

c

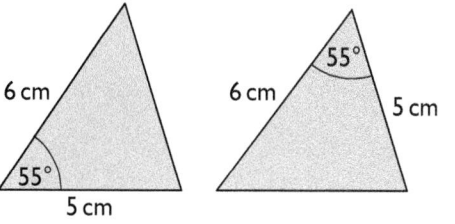

d

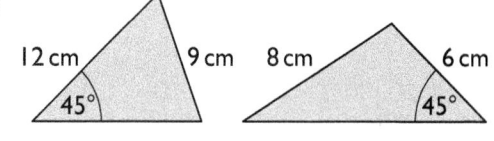

e

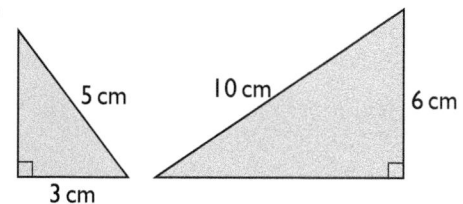

f

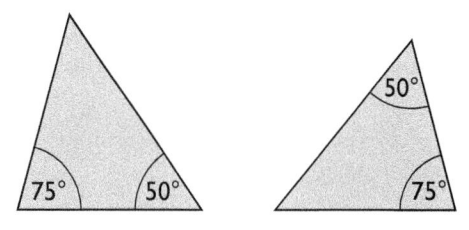

g

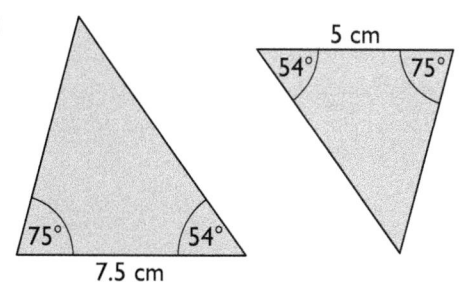

h

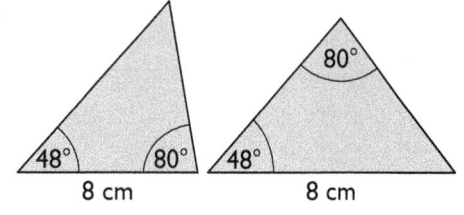

67

6 PQRS, WXY and DEF are parallel lines.
RX:XE = 2:3

   a Prove that triangles QRX and EFX are similar.

   b How many times longer is FQ than QX?

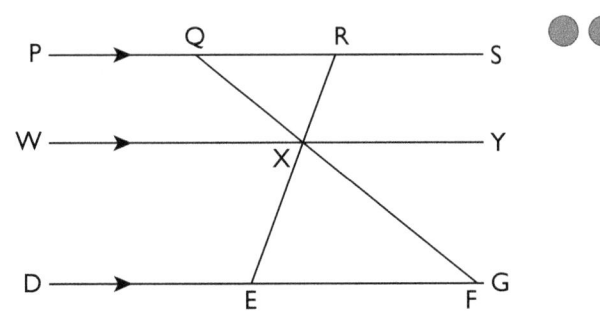

7 ABCD is a parallelogram.
The diagonals intersect at X.

   a Prove that triangles AXD and BXC are congruent.

   b Show that X is the mid-point of AC and BD.

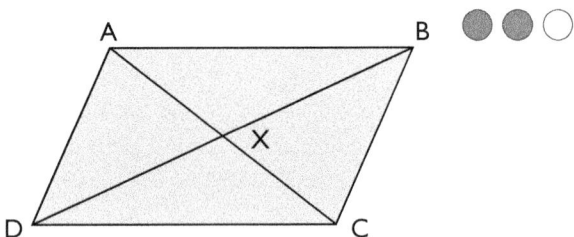

8 Show that PQ is parallel to RS.

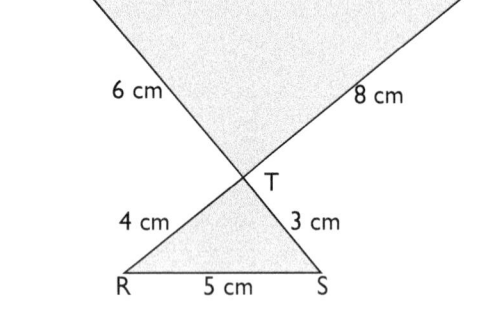

9 PQRT and UVST are parallelograms.
PUT, TSR and TVQ are straight lines.

   a Prove that triangle UVT is similar to triangle PQT.

   b Given that PU:UT = 2:3, find the value of QV:QT.

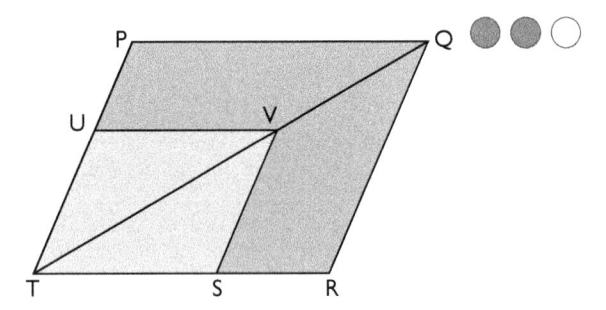

10 XZBC is a parallelogram.
AXC and AYB are straight lines.
AX:XC = 5:2.
Show that AY:AB = 5:7.

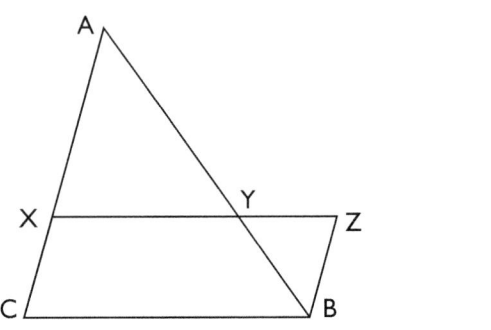

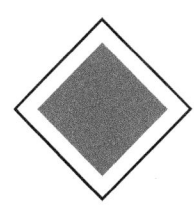

Geometry Strand 3
Measuring shapes Unit 5
Pythagoras' theorem

PS PRACTISING SKILLS **DF** DEVELOPING FLUENCY **PB** PROBLEM SOLVING **ES** EXAM-STYLE

PS 1 Work out the length of the hypotenuse in each triangle.
Give your answers correct to 1 decimal place.

a) 8 cm, 6 cm
b) 6 cm, 4 cm
c) 3 cm, 4.5 cm

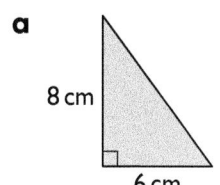

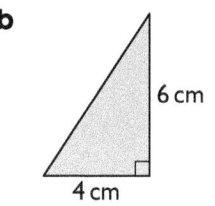

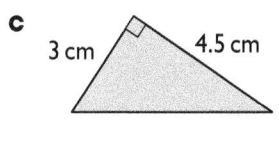

PS 2 Work out the length of the unknown side in each triangle.
Give your answer correct to 2 decimal places.

a) 6 cm, 8 cm
b) 6 cm, 4 cm
c) 3 cm, 4.5 cm

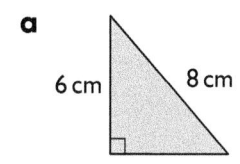

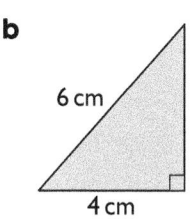

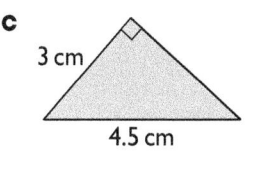

DF 3 Without using a calculator, work out the length of the unknown side in each triangle.

a) $\sqrt{5}$ cm, $\sqrt{11}$ cm
b) $\sqrt{35}$ cm, $\sqrt{10}$ cm
c) $\sqrt{44}$ cm, 12 cm

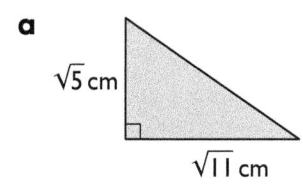

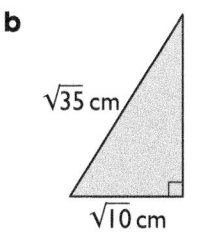

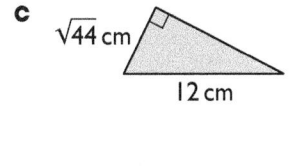

DF 4 Which of the three triangles are right-angled triangles?
Explain your answer.

a) 2 cm, 2.5 cm, 1.5 cm
b) 26 cm, 24.5 cm, 10 cm
c) 4.5 cm, 4.5 cm, 6.4 cm

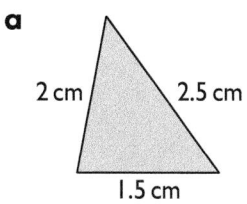

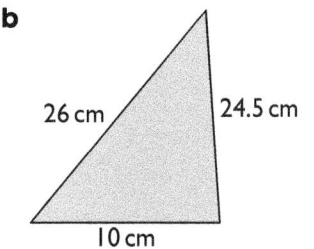

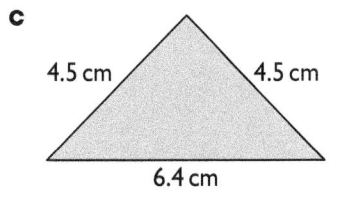

Geometry Strand 3 Measuring shapes Unit 5 Pythagoras' theorem

5 ABCD is a rectangle.

Work out the length of the diagonal BD.

Give your answer correct to 3 significant figures.

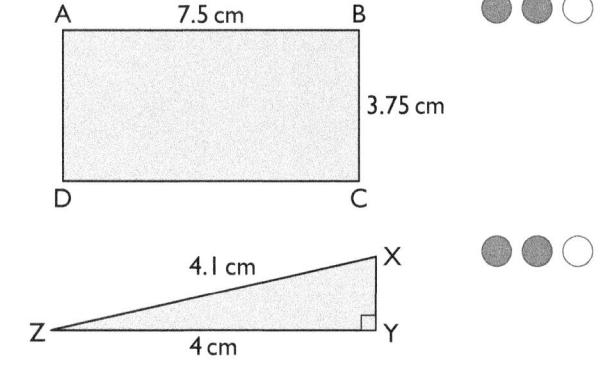

6 For triangle XYZ, work out

a the perimeter

b the area.

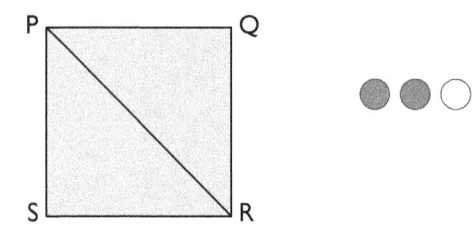

7 PQRS is a square. The diagonal is 16 cm.

Work out the perimeter of the square.

Give your answer correct to 3 significant figures.

8 A square is drawn with its vertices on the circumference of a circle. The diagonal of the square is 8 cm.

Work out the area of the shaded part of the diagram, giving your answer correct to 3 significant figures.

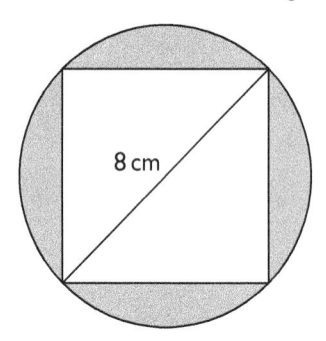

9 Calculate the area of the field shown in this diagram.

Give your answer in hectares to 3 significant figures.

(1 hectare = 10 000 m²)

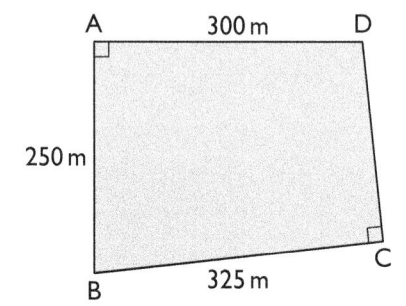

70

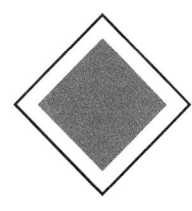

Geometry Strand 3
Measuring shapes
Unit 6 Arcs and sectors

PS — PRACTISING SKILLS   **DF** — DEVELOPING FLUENCY   **PB** — PROBLEM SOLVING   **ES** — EXAM-STYLE

PS 1 Calculate the lengths of these arcs.
Give your answers correct to 2 decimal places.

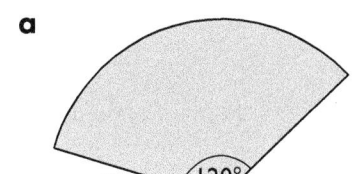

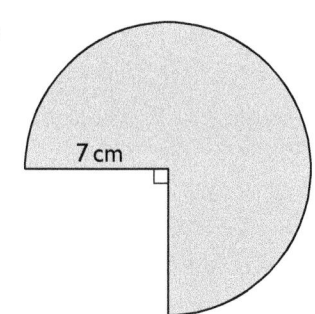

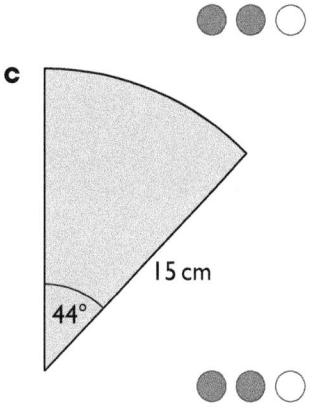

a) 5 cm, 120°
b) 7 cm (reflex, 270°)
c) 15 cm, 44°

PS 2 Calculate the areas of these sectors.
Give your answers correct to 1 decimal place.

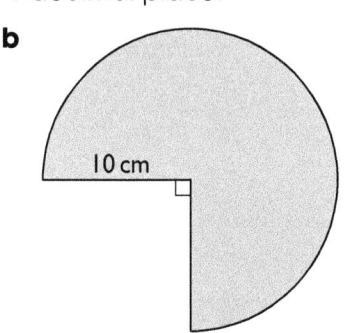

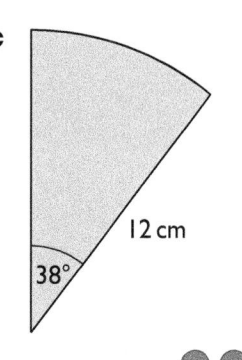

a) 8 cm, 130°
b) 10 cm (reflex, 270°)
c) 12 cm, 38°

DF 3 Work out the perimeter and area of each shape.
Give your answers correct to 3 significant figures.

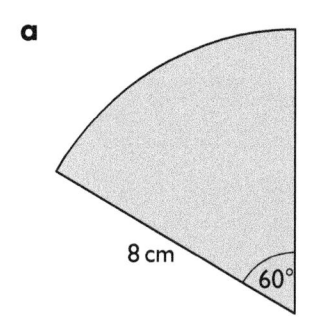

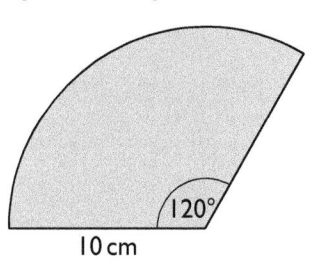

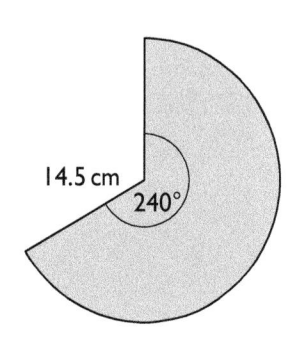

a) 8 cm, 60°
b) 10 cm, 120°
c) 14.5 cm, 240°

Geometry Strand 3 Measuring shapes Unit 6 Arcs and sectors

DF 4 The shaded part of this diagram shows the throwing area of a sports field.
Calculate the area.
Give your answer to the nearest whole number.

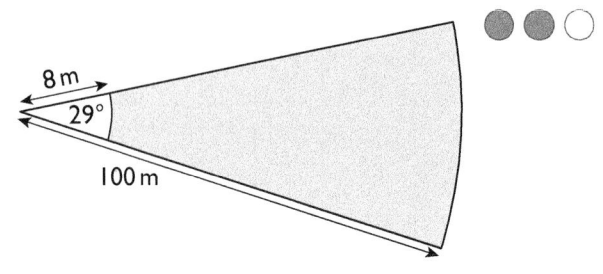

DF 5 A sector has a radius of 7.5 cm and an area of 25π cm².
Calculate the angle at the centre.

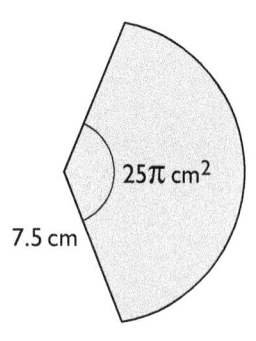

DF 6 A sector arc has length of 20π cm and an angle of 100°.
Calculate the radius of the sector.

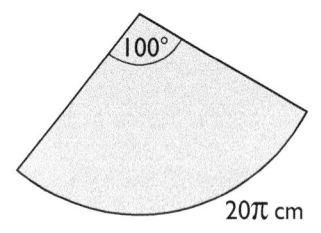

PB 7 The arc length of a sector is the same as its radius.
ES What is the angle at the centre?
Give your answer correct to 3 significant figures.

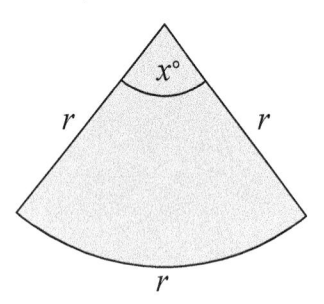

Geometry Strand 3 Measuring shapes Unit 6 Arcs and sectors

8 The diagram represents the design for a bread bin.

The cross-section of the prism is a quarter circle of radius 20 cm.

The length of the bread bin is 35 cm.

Work out the volume of this bread bin, giving your answer correct to 3 significant figures.

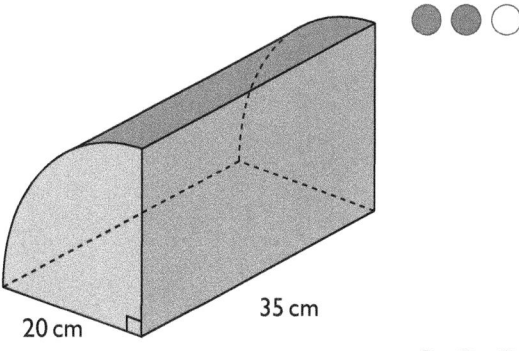

9 The diagram represents the plan for a flower bed.

The flower bed is the region between 2 semicircles. The semicircles have the same centre, S.

Percy wants to put edging strips along each edge of the flower bed.

He has 15 lengths of edging strip. Each length is 1.5 m.

Does Percy have enough edging strip?

Show your working.

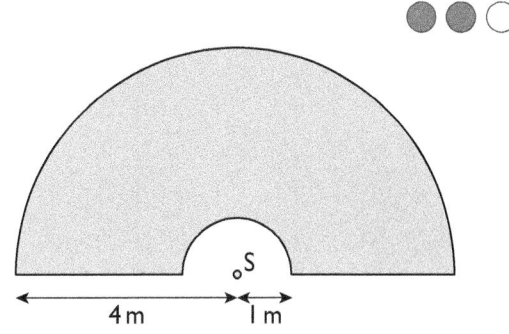

10 The diagram shows the design for a brooch.

The brooch has diameter 2.5 cm and will be made from three different metals.

The area of the gold, silver and copper sectors are in the ratio 4 : 3 : 1.

Work out the total area of the silver sectors, giving your answer correct to 1 decimal place.

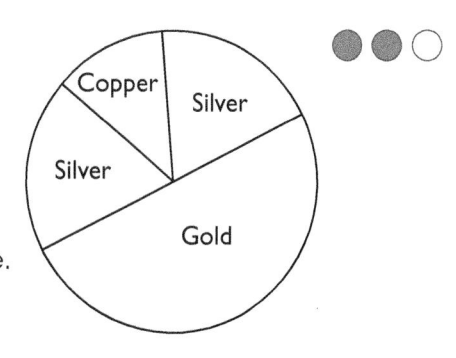

11 Work out the area that is shaded.

Give your answer in terms of π.

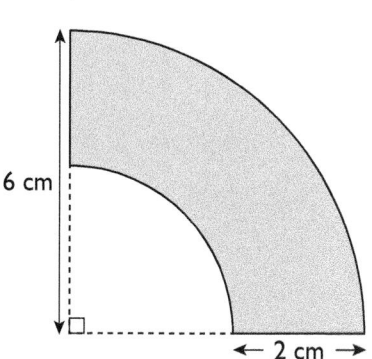

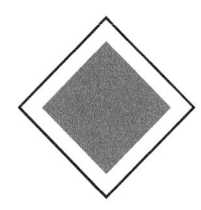

Geometry Strand 4
Construction Unit 3
Constructions with a pair of compasses

PS PRACTISING SKILLS   **DF** DEVELOPING FLUENCY   **PB** PROBLEM SOLVING   **ES** EXAM-STYLE

PS 1 Use a ruler and a pair of compasses to construct each triangle accurately.

a 6 cm, 7 cm, 5 cm

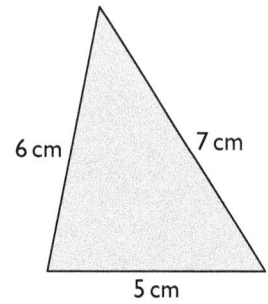

b 5 cm, 4 cm, 5 cm

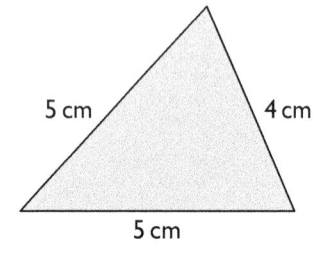

c 7 cm, 10 cm, 5 cm

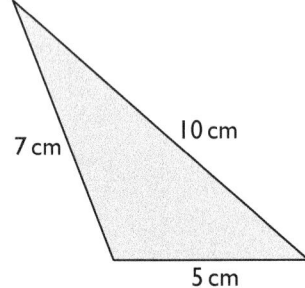

PS 2 Use a ruler and a protractor to construct each triangle accurately.

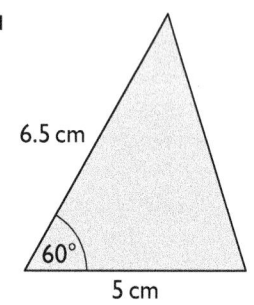

a 6.5 cm, 60°, 5 cm

b 5.6 cm, 60°, 4.5 cm

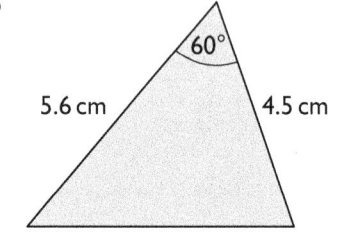

c 6 cm, 120°, 5 cm

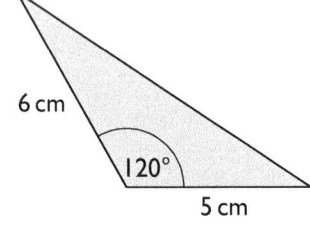

PS 3 Draw these triangles accurately.

a 60°, 35°, 5.7 cm

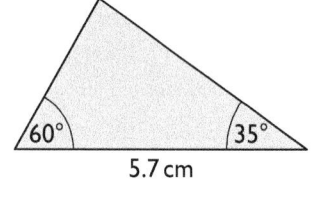

b 40°, 7.5 cm, right angle

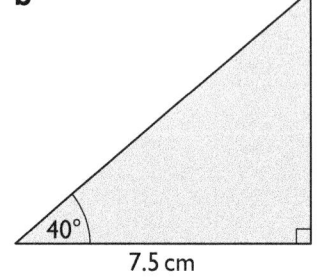

c 10 cm, 60°, 5 cm

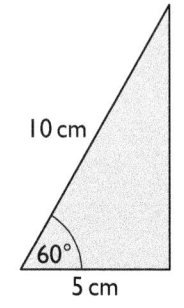

Geometry Strand 4 Construction Unit 3 Constructions with a pair of compasses

PS **4** Use a ruler and a pair of compasses to construct each angle.
  a 90°
  b 120°
  c 45°
  d 30°

DF **5** **a** Use a ruler and a pair of compasses to construct triangle ABC.
  b Construct the perpendicular bisector of each of the three sides.
  c Mark the point M where the three perpendicular bisectors meet.
  d Draw a circle with centre M that passes through the points A, B, and C. This is called the circumscribed circle of the triangle.

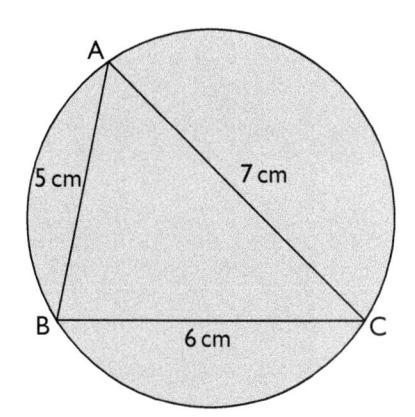

DF **6** **a** Use a ruler and a pair of compasses to construct triangle PQR.
  b Construct the angle bisector of each of the three angles.
  c Mark the point M where the three angle bisectors meet.
  d Draw a circle with centre M that touches the sides PQ, QR, and PR. This is called the inscribed circle of the triangle.

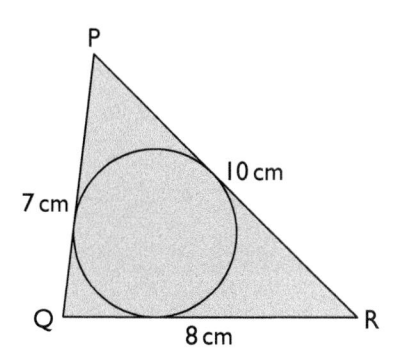

Geometry Strand 4 Construction Unit 3 Constructions with a pair of compasses

7 a Use a ruler and a pair of compasses to construct triangle DEF.
   b Bisect the exterior angles BDE and GED.
   c Mark the point M where the angle bisectors meet.
   d Draw a circle with centre M to touch BD, DE and EG.
      This is called an escribed circle of the triangle.

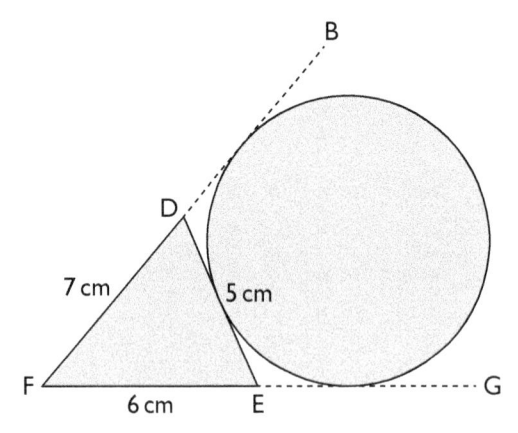

8 a Use a ruler and a pair of compasses to construct a quadrilateral ABCD inscribed in a circle of radius 5 cm so that:
   - AB = 5 cm
   - BC = 7 cm
   - angle BAD = 90°.
   b What part of the circle is the diagonal BD?

9 a Use a ruler and a pair of compasses to construct a triangle PQR with PQ = 8 cm, QR = 6.8 cm and angle PQR = 45°.
   b Mark the point A on PQ so that PA = AQ.
   c Construct a rectangle ABCD so that B lies on PR and both C and D lie on QR.

10 ABCD is a quadrilateral.
   AB = BC = 6 cm
   AD = 10 cm
   Angle A = 60°
   Angle B = 135°

   a Construct the perpendiculars from B and C onto AD.
   b Hence find the area of ABCD.

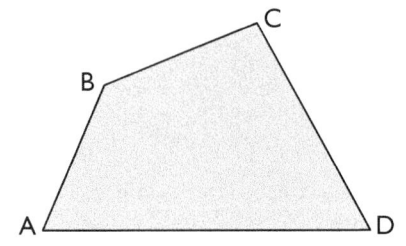

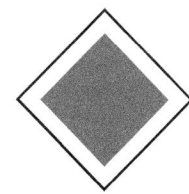

Geometry Strand 4
Construction Unit 4 Loci

PS PRACTISING SKILLS   **DF** DEVELOPING FLUENCY   **PB** PROBLEM SOLVING   **ES** EXAM-STYLE

DF 1 Draw a co-ordinate grid on 2 mm graph paper.
Draw the x-axis from –6 to 6.
Draw the y-axis from –5 to 7.
Draw the locus of the points that are

  a 4 cm from (1, 1)

  b 2 cm from the line joining (–3, 3) and (–3, –2)

  c the same distance from the points (1, 5) and (5, 1)

  d the same distance from the lines joining (–4, 4) to (0, –4) and (0, 4) to (–4, –4).

DF 2 Copy the co-ordinate grid from question **1** on to squared paper.
Draw the locus of the points that are

  a at most 3 cm from (–2, 2)

  b 2 cm from the line joining (–2, –3) to (2, –3)

  c closer to the line joining the points (1, 5) and (–4, 0) than the line joining the points (5, 1) and (–4, 0).

PB 3 The diagram shows Alice's garden.
Alice wants to plant a new tree in her garden.
The tree will be planted:

  • nearer to RQ than RS

  • more than 10 m from PS

  • less than 8 m from Q.

  a Draw the diagram accurately, using a scale of 1 cm = 2 m.

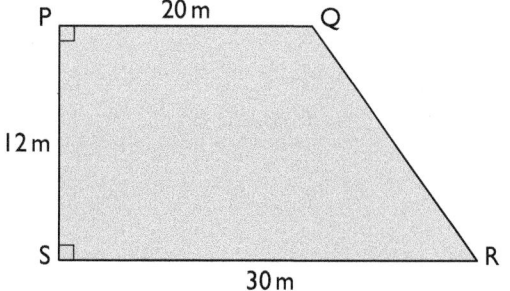

  b Shade the region where Alice could plant her new tree.

Geometry Strand 4 Construction Unit 4 Loci

4 The diagram shows the positions of Colchester and Ipswich.
Ipswich is 18 miles north east of Colchester.
A company want to build a new hotel such that

- it is nearer Ipswich than Colchester
- it is less than 12 miles from Colchester.

a Draw the diagram accurately, using a scale of 1 cm = 2 miles.

b Shade the region where the hotel could be built.

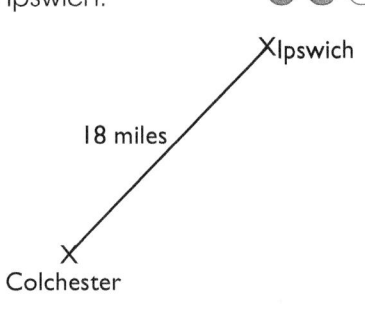

5 The diagram shows a car park that measures 75 m by 55 m.
Cars must not be parked within 20 m of W or within 15 m of XY.

a Draw the car park accurately, using a scale of 1 cm = 10 m.

b Shade the region where the cars should not be parked.

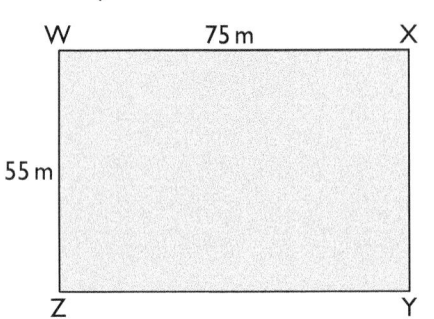

6 PQRS is a square piece of card placed on a straight line.

The card is first rotated 90° clockwise about R.
It is then rotated 90° clockwise about Q.
Finally it is rotated 90° clockwise about P.
Draw the locus of the vertex S.

78

7 In the diagram:
- P and Q are buoys.
  P is 750 m due North of Q and Q is 1 km NE of H.
- H is 1 km on a bearing of 020° from R.

Pete has to steer his boat along a course from port R between the buoys at P and Q. He must stay at least 300 m away from H.

He wants to sail due North from R and then onto a course on the perpendicular bisector of P and Q.

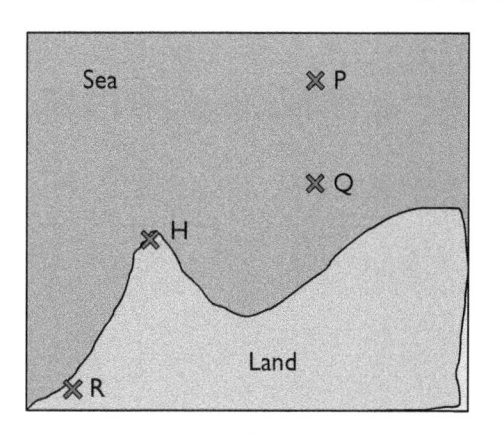

a Draw an accurate diagram of Pete's boat trip, using a scale of 1 cm = 100 m.

b Will he pass too close to H?
Explain your answer.

8 The diagram shows a triangular tile, ABC, which is placed on a table.
A piece of string of length 10 cm is attached to A.
The string is held taut and rotated clockwise around the triangle.
Draw the locus of the point P.

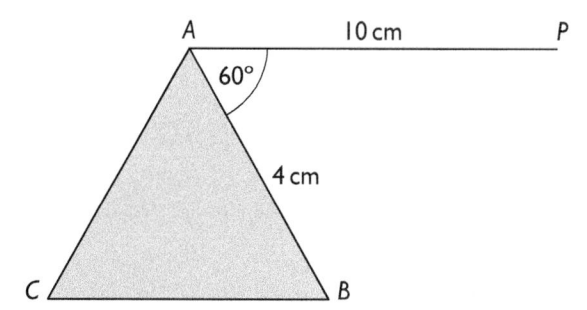

9 The diagram shows the locus of a point on the circumference of a bicycle wheel as it moves in a straight line.

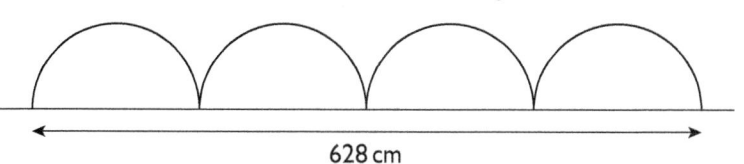

628 cm

What is the diameter of the bicycle wheel?
Give your answer to the nearest centimetre.

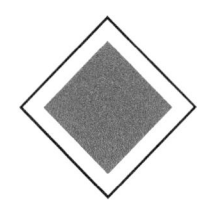

Geometry Strand 5
Transformations Unit 7
Similarity

PS PRACTISING SKILLS   **DF** DEVELOPING FLUENCY   **PB** PROBLEM SOLVING   **ES** EXAM-STYLE

PS 1 Work out the lettered lengths in each pair of similar triangles.

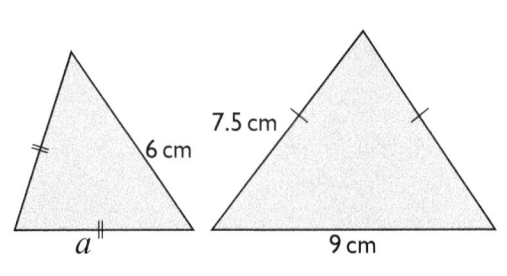

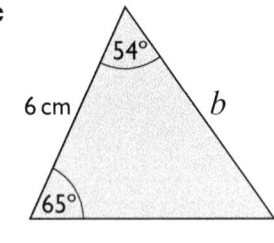

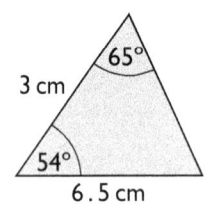

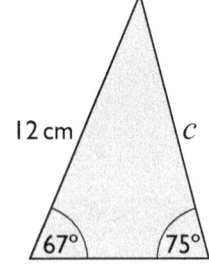

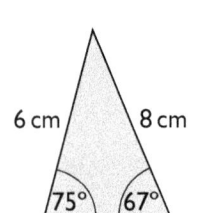

a 5 cm, 5 cm, 70°, x ; 12 cm, 10 cm, 70°, y

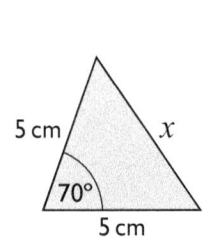

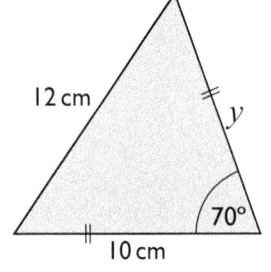

b 6 cm, a ; 7.5 cm, 9 cm

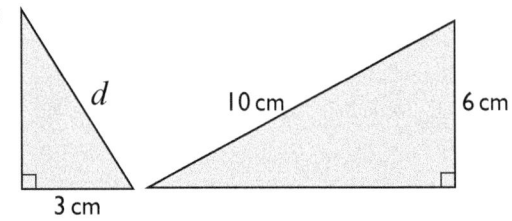

c 54°, 6 cm, 65°, b ; 3 cm, 65°, 54°, 6.5 cm

d 12 cm, 67°, 75°, c ; 6 cm, 8 cm, 75°, 67°

e d, 3 cm ; 10 cm, 6 cm

f 75°, 50°, 12.5 cm, e ; 6 cm, 50°, 5 cm, 75°

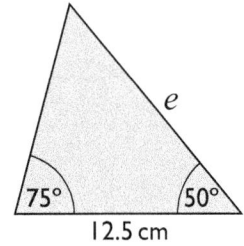

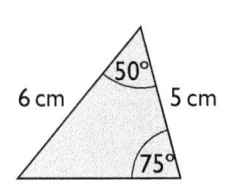

PS 2 XYZ and PQR are two similar triangles. Work out the length of

a XY

b PR.

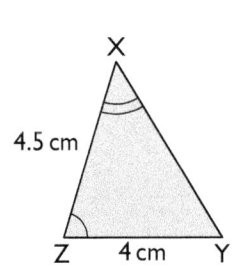

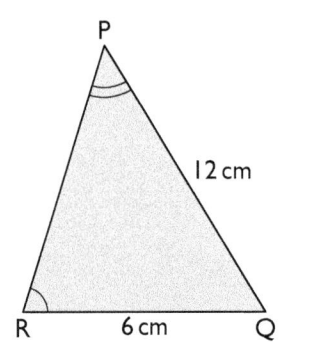

X: 4.5 cm, Z, 4 cm, Y
P: 12 cm, R, 6 cm, Q

Geometry Strand 5 Transformations Unit 7 Similarity

DF **3** Work out the lettered lengths in each pair of similar shapes.

a

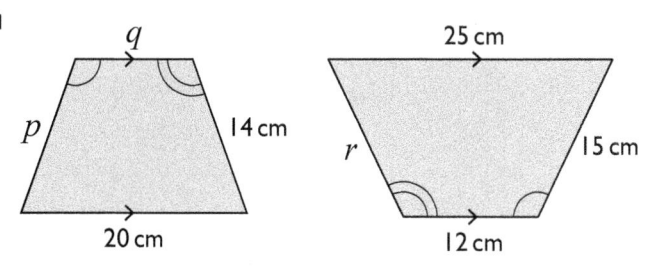

q = (top of left shape), p = (left side), 14 cm, 20 cm; 25 cm, r, 15 cm, 12 cm

b

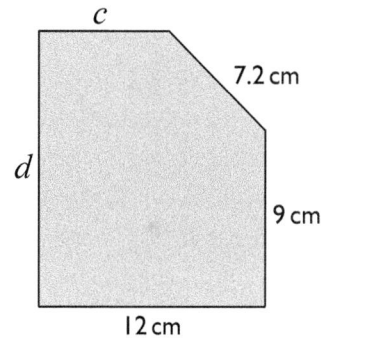

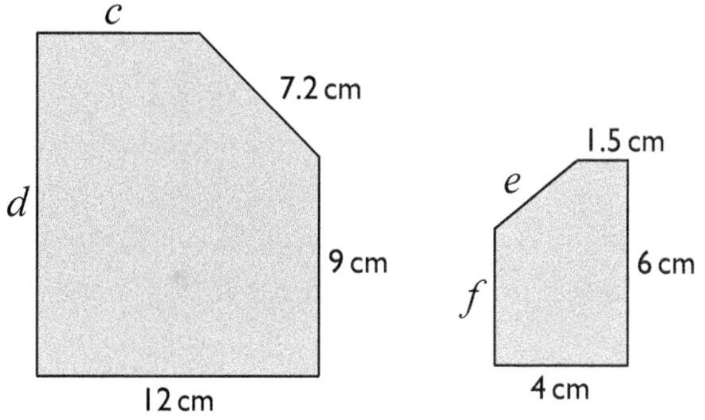

c, 7.2 cm, d, 9 cm, 12 cm; 1.5 cm, e, 6 cm, f, 4 cm

DF **ES** **4** Triangles ABX and QPX are similar.
Work out the length of
 a AX
 b PX.

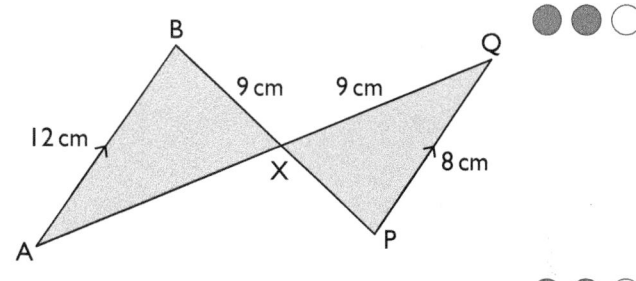

(BX = 9 cm, XQ = 9 cm, AB = 12 cm, PQ = 8 cm)

DF **ES** **5** ABC and ADE are two similar triangles.
BC is parallel to DE.
Work out the length of
 a BC
 b AE.

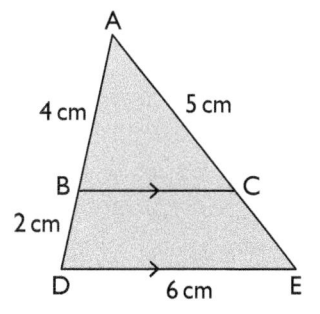

(AB = 4 cm, AC = 5 cm, BD = 2 cm, DE = 6 cm)

DF **ES** **6** Triangles DEF and HGJ are similar.
Work out the length of
 a DE
 b JH.

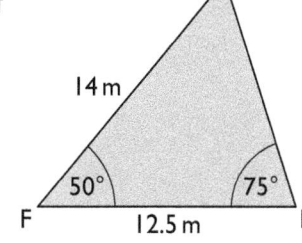

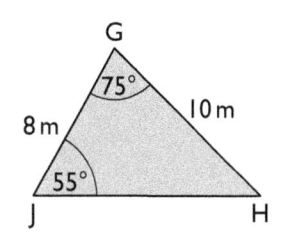

(DF = 14 m, FE = 12.5 m, angle F = 50°, angle E = 75°; G = 75°, GH = 10 m, JG = 8 m, angle J = 55°)

81

Geometry Strand 5 Transformations Unit 7 Similarity

7 In this diagram, PQ is parallel to RS.
Work out the length of
   a RT
   b PT.

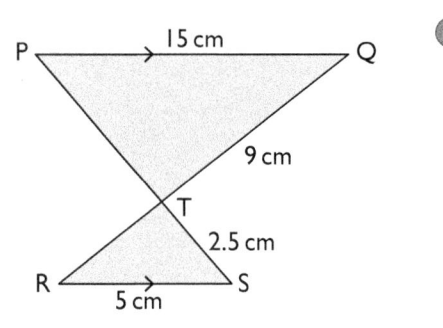

8 PQRT and UVST are parallelograms.
PUT, TSR and TVQ are straight lines.
PQ = 21 cm
SV = 15 cm
PU : UT = 1 : 2
Work out the length of
   a UV
   b QR.

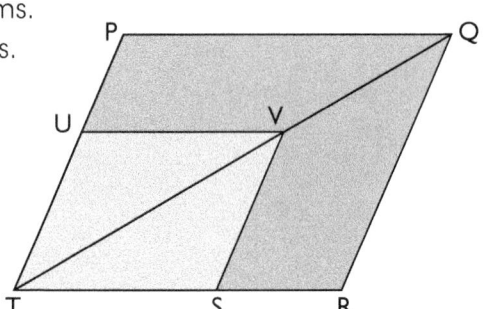

9 The diagram shows a set of supports of two sizes made to support shelves.
Work out the value of
   a x
   b y.

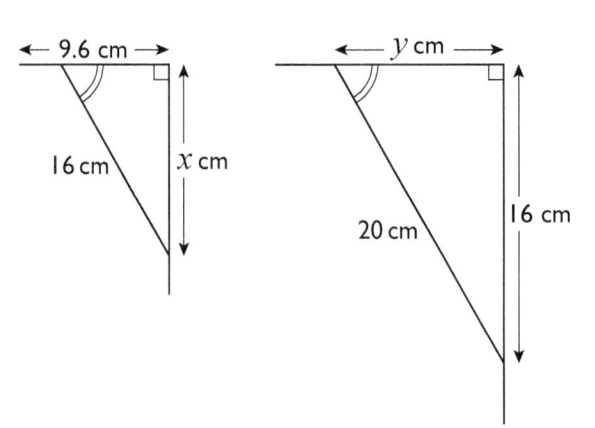

10 The diagram shows part of a structure for a building.
The angles are marked on the diagram.
CH, DG and EF are parallel.
   a What is the size of angle QDA?
BC = CD = DE = 12 m   and   DG = 20 m
   b Work out the length of
       i CH
       ii EF.

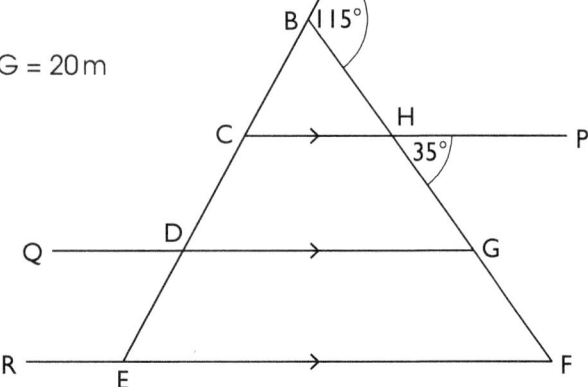

82

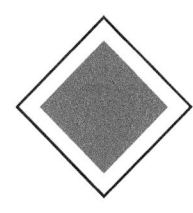

Geometry Strand 5
Transformations Unit 8
Trigonometry

PS — PRACTISING SKILLS   **DF** — DEVELOPING FLUENCY   **PB** — PROBLEM SOLVING   **ES** — EXAM-STYLE

PS / ES 1 Work out the length of the lettered side in each right-angled triangle. Give your answers correct to 1 decimal place.

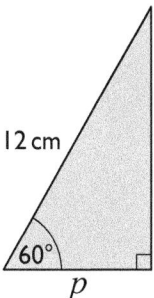

a) 12 cm, 60°, side p

b) q, 50°, 8 cm

c) 55°, 15 cm, r

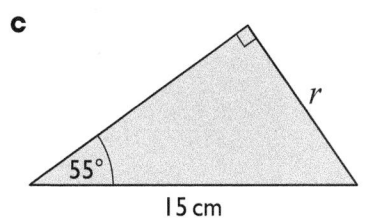

PS / ES 2 For each triangle, work out the value of θ. Give your answer correct to 1 decimal place.

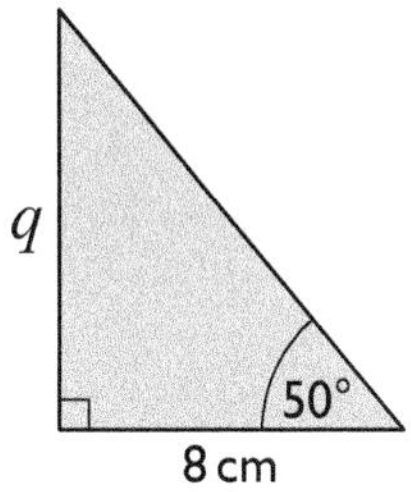

a) 6 cm, 8 cm, θ

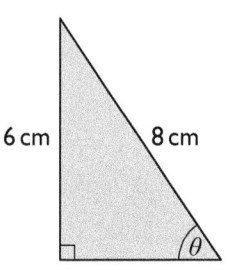

b) 6 cm, 4 cm, θ

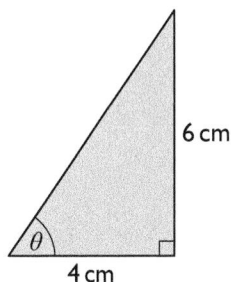

c) 3 cm, 4.5 cm, θ

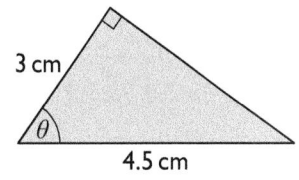

PS / ES 3 Work out the length of the lettered side in each right-angled triangle. Give your answers correct to 2 decimal places.

a) 10 cm, 60°, d

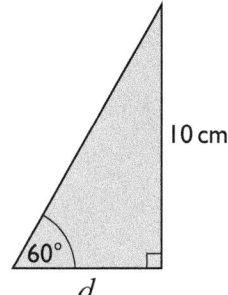

b) 35°, e, 6.5 cm

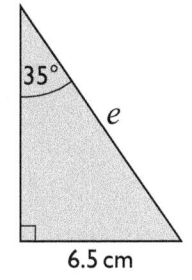

c) 12.5 cm, 28°, f

83

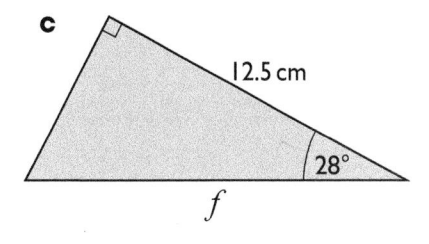

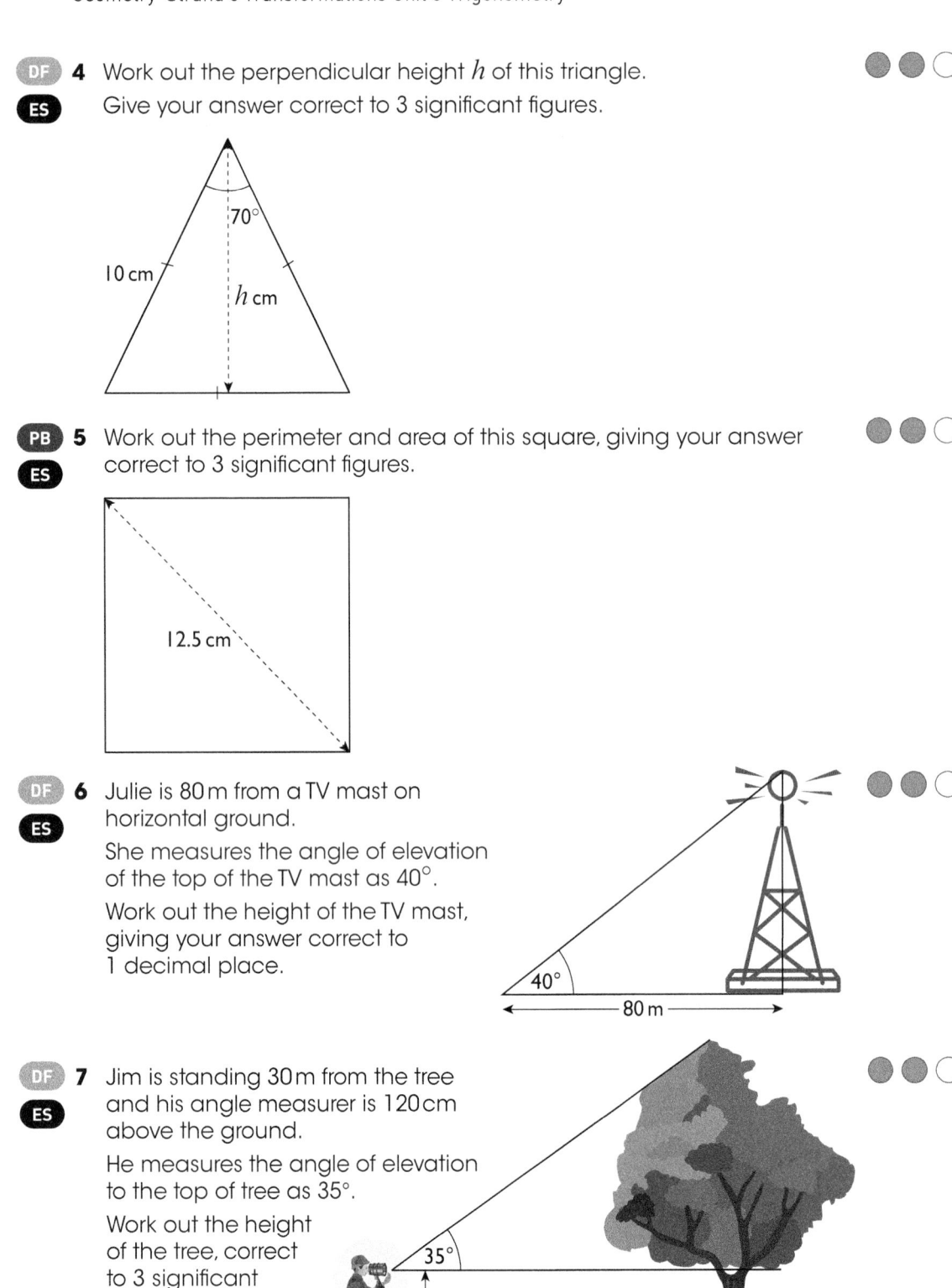

Geometry Strand 5 Transformations Unit 8 Trigonometry

DF **4** Work out the perpendicular height h of this triangle.
ES Give your answer correct to 3 significant figures.

PB **5** Work out the perimeter and area of this square, giving your answer
ES correct to 3 significant figures.

DF **6** Julie is 80 m from a TV mast on horizontal ground.
ES She measures the angle of elevation of the top of the TV mast as 40°.

Work out the height of the TV mast, giving your answer correct to 1 decimal place.

DF **7** Jim is standing 30 m from the tree and his angle measurer is 120 cm above the ground.
ES

He measures the angle of elevation to the top of tree as 35°.

Work out the height of the tree, correct to 3 significant figures.

84

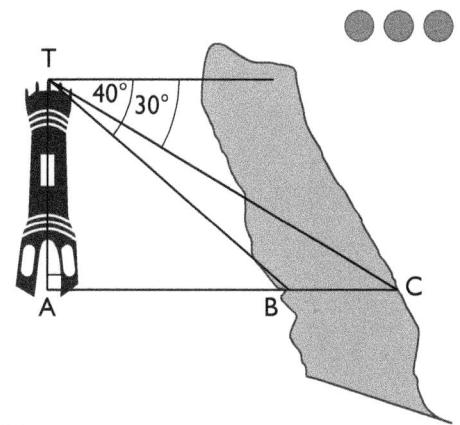

Geometry Strand 5 Transformations Unit 8 Trigonometry

PB ES 8 The diagram shows a framework made from five rods.

The rectangle has a length of 12 m.

The diagonal makes an angle of 25° with the base of the rectangle.

Work out the total length of the five rods in the framework.

Give your answer correct to 3 significant figures.

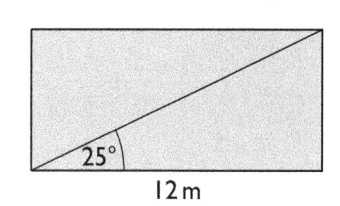

PB ES 9 The longest diagonal of a rhombus is 10 cm.

This diagonal makes an angle of 30° with the base of the rhombus.

Work out the perimeter of the rhombus, giving your answer correct to 3 significant figures.

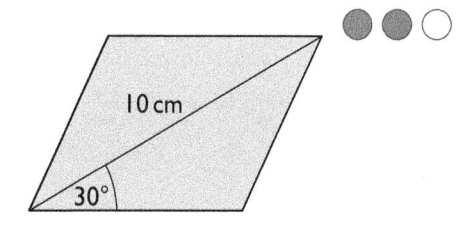

PB ES 10 Alfie takes his boat to check two offshore windmills at W and M.

He leaves the harbour H and travels due East for 12 km to W and then 5 km due North to M.

On what bearing must he travel to get directly back to H?

Give your answer to the nearest degree.

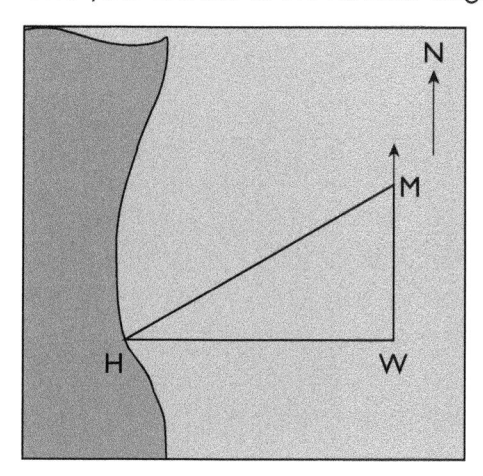

PB ES 11 Kirsty wants to find the width of a river.

She stands at the top of the tower, T. The base of the tower is at A.

ABC is a straight line.

Angle TAB is a right angle.

The angle of depression of:

- B from T is 40°
- C from T is 30°.

The base of the tower is 100 m from B.

Work out the width of the river.

Give your answer correct to 3 significant figures.

85

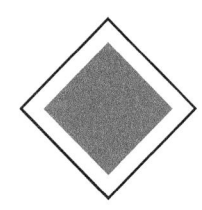

Geometry Strand 5
Transformations
Unit 9 Trigonometry for special angles

PS — PRACTISING SKILLS   **DF** — DEVELOPING FLUENCY   **PB** — PROBLEM SOLVING   **ES** — EXAM-STYLE

PS 1 Work out the exact length of the lettered side in each triangle.

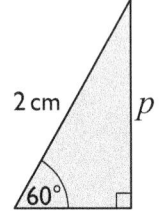

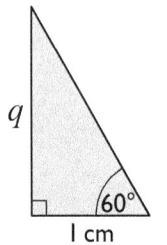

a. Triangle with 2 cm side, 60° angle, side p, right angle.

b. Triangle with side q, 60° angle, 1 cm base, right angle.

c. Right-angled triangle with side r, 60° angle, 2 cm.

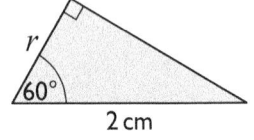

PS 2 Work out the size of θ in each triangle.

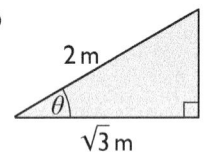

a. Triangle with 5 cm, 5 cm, angle θ, right angle.

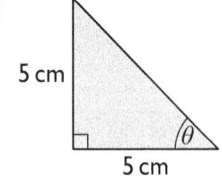

b. Triangle with 2 m, $\sqrt{3}$ m, angle θ, right angle.

c. Triangle with 3 cm, 6 cm, angle θ, right angle.

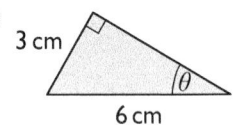

PS 3 Work out the exact length of the lettered side in each triangle.

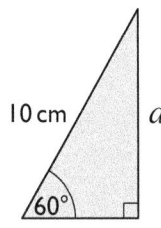

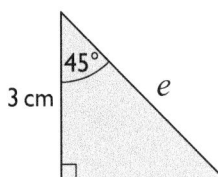

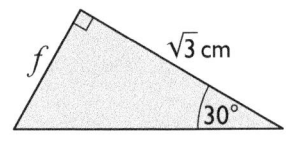

a. Triangle with 10 cm, 60° angle, side d, right angle.

b. Triangle with 45° angle, 3 cm, side e, right angle.

c. Triangle with side f, $\sqrt{3}$ cm, 30° angle, right angle.

PB **4** Calculate the exact area of this triangle.
ES

Triangle with 20 cm, 45° angle, right angle.

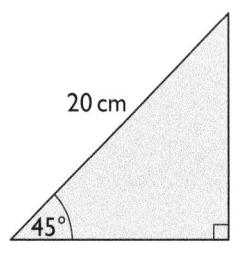

Geometry Strand 5 Transformations Unit 9 Trigonometry for special angles

PB **ES** **5** Show that the exact value of the area of this equilateral triangle is $64\sqrt{3}$ cm².

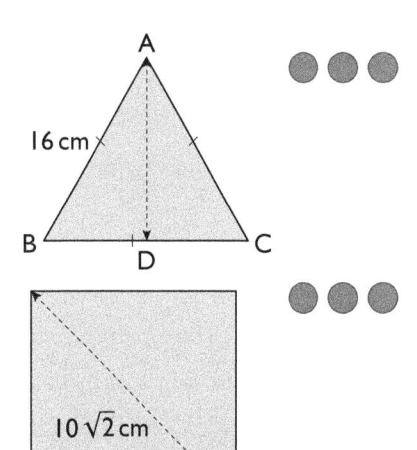

16 cm

PB **ES** **6** Work out the perimeter and area of a square that has a diagonal of length $10\sqrt{2}$ cm.

$10\sqrt{2}$ cm

PB **ES** **7** The longest diagonal of a rhombus is $10\sqrt{3}$ cm.
This diagonal makes an angle of 30° with the base of the rhombus.

$10\sqrt{3}$ cm

30°

  a Work out the perimeter of the rhombus.
  b Prove that the area of the rhombus is $50\sqrt{3}$ cm².

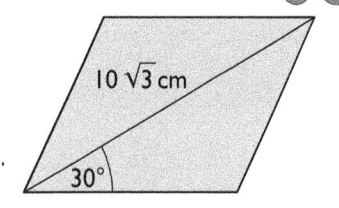

PB **ES** **8** The diagram shows a regular octagon of side $8\sqrt{2}$ cm.
Show that the area of the octagon is $256(1 + \sqrt{2})$ cm².

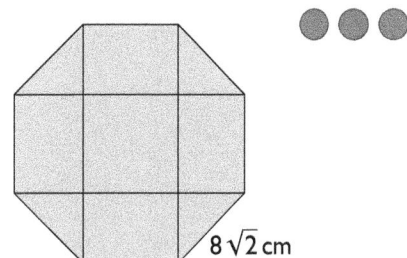

$8\sqrt{2}$ cm

PB **ES** **9** This logo is made from two grey right-angled isosceles triangles and a white equilateral triangle.
The equilateral triangle has sides of length 2 m.

  a Work out the area of the logo.
  b What is the perimeter of the logo?

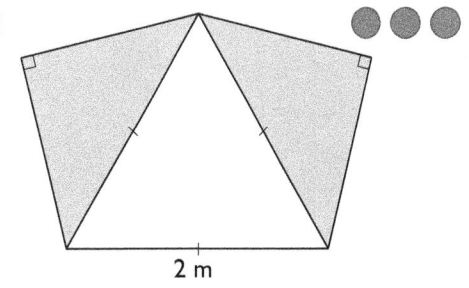

2 m

PB **ES** **10** Leo makes a stained glass light-catcher by putting a regular hexagon within a rectangle within a circle.
The length of each side of the hexagon is 10 cm.
Work out the length of the diameter of the circle.

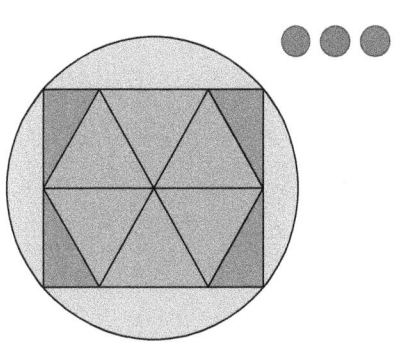

87

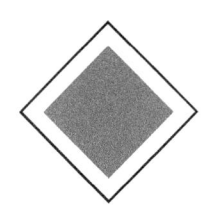

Geometry Strand 5
Transformations
Unit 10 Finding centres of rotation

PS PRACTISING SKILLS **DF** DEVELOPING FLUENCY **PB** PROBLEM SOLVING **ES** EXAM-STYLE

PS **1** Copy the diagram. Write down the centre and angle of rotation for

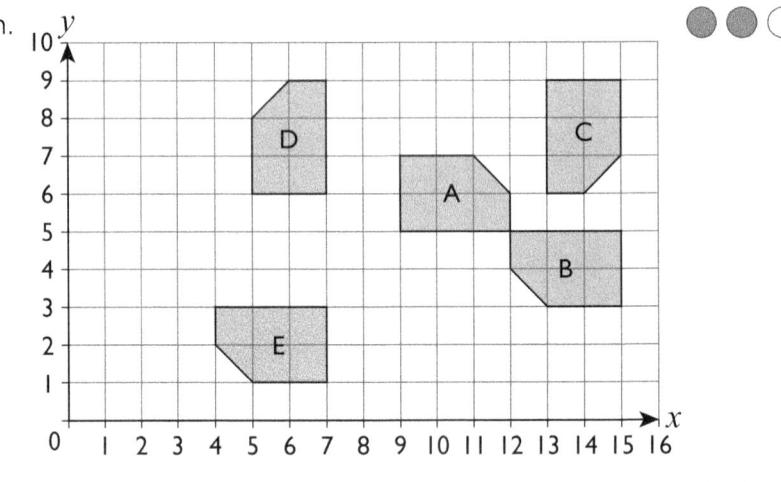

  a A → B
  b A → C
  c A → D
  d A → E.

PS **2** Write down the centre and angle of the rotation that transforms triangle P onto

  a triangle A
  b triangle B
  c triangle C.

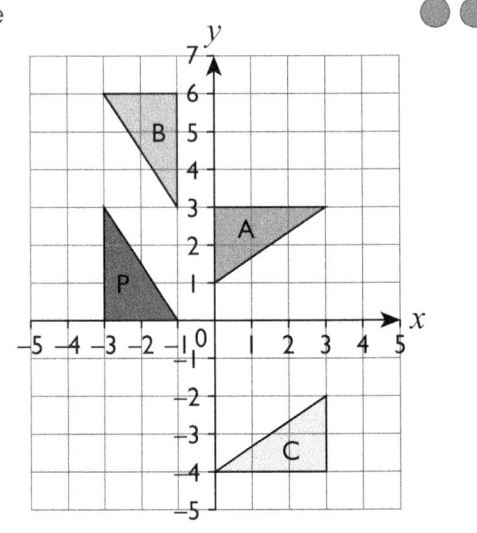

3 Look at the diagram in question **2**. Describe fully the rotations that map

   a triangle A onto triangle C

   b triangle B onto triangle A

   c triangle C onto triangle P

   d triangle B onto triangle C.

4 a Describe fully the rotations that map shape S to

   i shape A

   ii shape B

   iii shape C.

  b Explain why shape D is not a rotation of shape S.

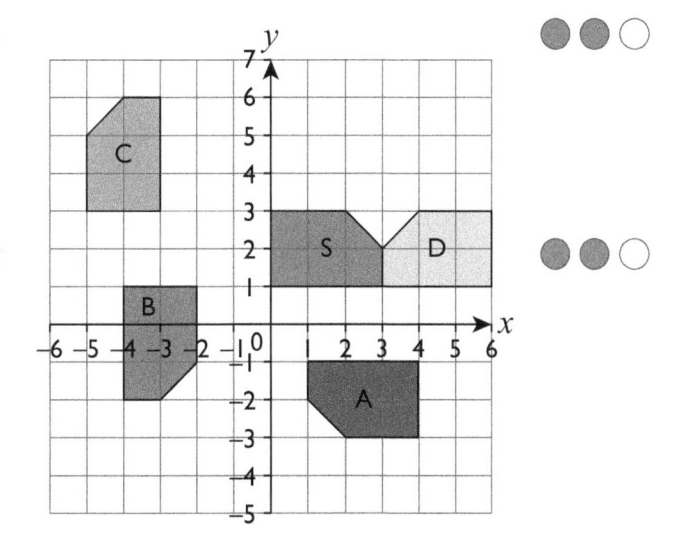

5 a Reflect triangle P in the line $x = -2$. Label the new triangle Q.

  b Reflect triangle Q in the line $y = 1$. Label the new triangle R.

  c Describe fully the single transformation that maps triangle P directly to triangle R.

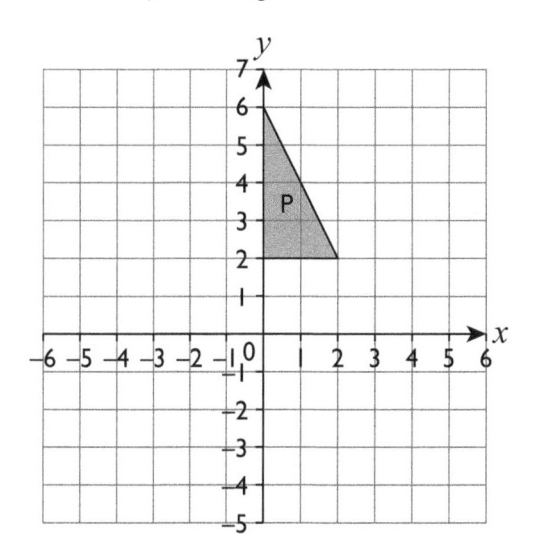

Geometry Strand 5 Transformations Unit 10 Finding centres of rotation

6 **a** Reflect triangle T in the line $x = 0$. Label the new triangle U.
  b Translate triangle U by the vector $\begin{pmatrix} 4 \\ -2 \end{pmatrix}$. Label the new triangle V.
  c Reflect triangle V in the line $y = -1$. Label the new triangle W.
  d Describe fully the single transformation that maps triangle T directly to triangle W.

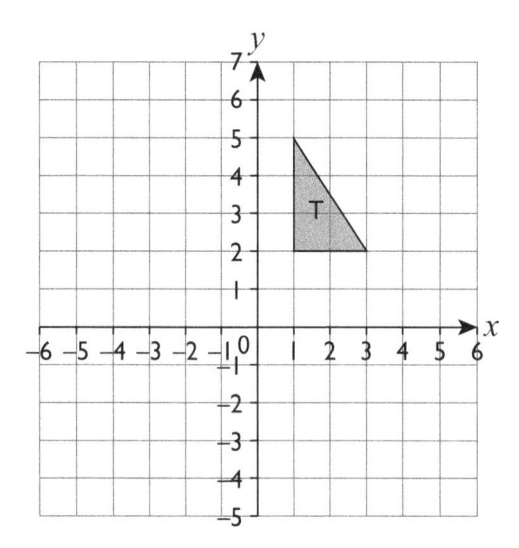

7 Shape P is reflected in the line with equation $y = x + 1$ to give shape Q. Shape Q is reflected in the line $y = x - 2$ to give shape R.
Describe fully the single transformation that maps shape R directly to shape P.

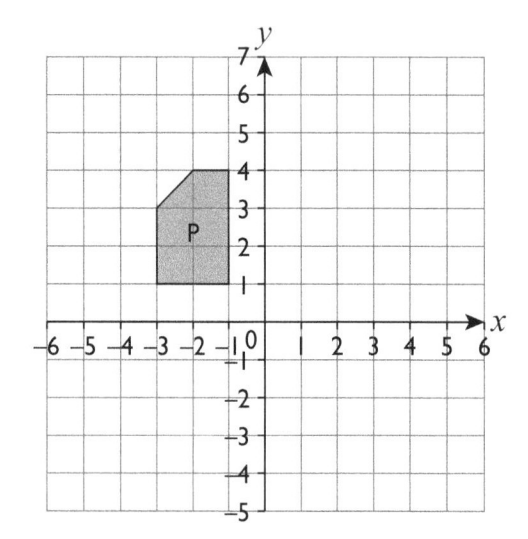

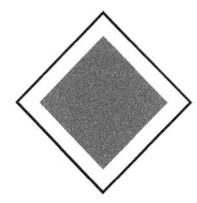

Geometry Strand 6 Three-dimensional shapes
Unit 7 Constructing plans and elevations

PS PRACTISING SKILLS   **DF** DEVELOPING FLUENCY   **PB** PROBLEM SOLVING   **ES** EXAM-STYLE

PS **1** Sketch the plan, front elevation and side elevation of these shapes.

a   b 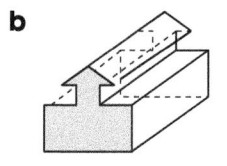   c 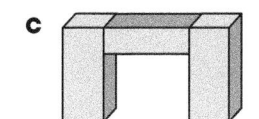   d

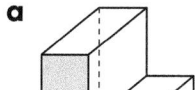

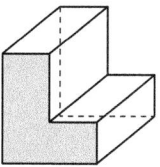

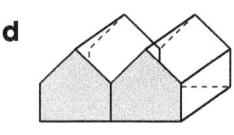

PS **2** The diagram shows the plan and elevations of a plinth.
Make an isometric drawing of this shape.

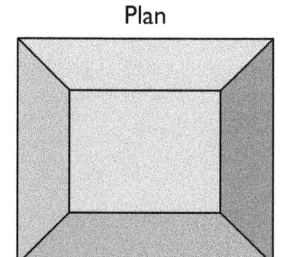

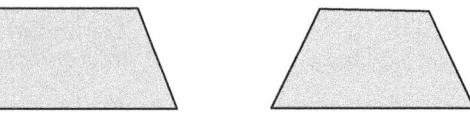

Plan   Front elevation   Side elevation

DF **3** The diagram shows a building.
ES Draw the plan, front elevation and side elevation.

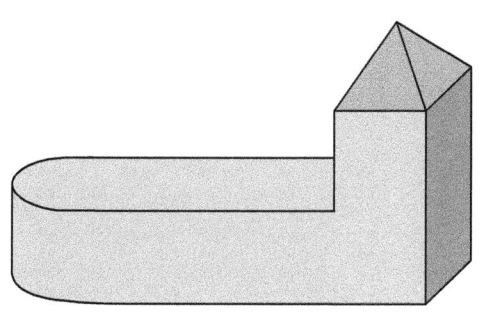

Geometry Strand 6 Three-dimensional shapes Unit 7 Constructing plans and elevations

4 The diagram shows Emma's workshop.
The apex of the roof is central to the base.
The maximum height of the workshop is 3.5 m.
Draw an appropriate elevation to scale and use it to work out the area of the roof of the workshop.

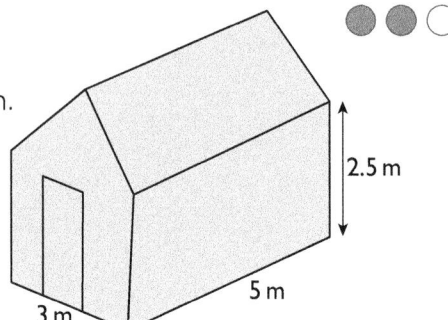

2.5 m
5 m
3 m

5 The diagram shows an isometric scale drawing of a 3D shape.
The isometric grid is made with 1 cm triangles. 1 cm represents 5 cm.

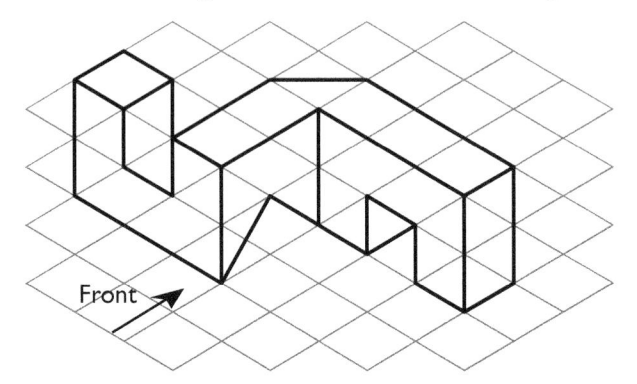

Front

Make an accurate drawing of the plan, front elevation and side elevation of the shape.

6 Here are the plan and elevations of a structure made from toy building bricks.
The structure is made from:
- two cuboids with a square cross-section of side 4 cm and height 2 cm
- one cuboid with a square cross-section of side 2 cm and length 4 cm
- a square-based pyramid with a vertical height of 2 cm.

Draw the 3D shape on isometric paper.

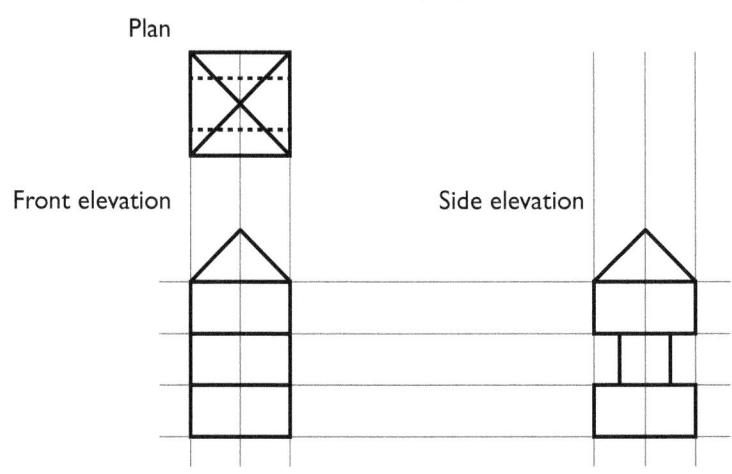

Plan

Front elevation   Side elevation

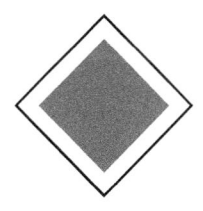

Geometry Strand 6 Three-dimensional shapes
Unit 8 Surface area and volume of 3D shapes

PS — PRACTISING SKILLS   **DF** — DEVELOPING FLUENCY   **PB** — PROBLEM SOLVING   **ES** — EXAM-STYLE

Surface area of a sphere = $4\pi r^2$

Curved surface area of a cone = $\pi r l$

Volume of a sphere = $\frac{4}{3}\pi r^3$

Volume of a cone = $\frac{1}{3}\pi r^2 h$

Volume of a pyramid = $\frac{1}{3}$ × area of a base × height

PS **1** Calculate the volume and surface area of a sphere with
   a radius 4 cm
   b diameter 7 cm.
   Give your answers correct to 3 significant figures.

PS **2** Work out the volume and curved surface area of a cone with
   a radius 5 cm, vertical height 12 cm, slant height 13 cm
   b diameter 12 cm, vertical height 8 cm, slant height 10 cm.
   Give your answers correct to 3 significant figures.

DF ES **3** A sphere has volume 36π cm³.
   Calculate the radius of the sphere.

DF ES **4** A cone with a slant height of 10 cm has surface area 40π cm².
   Work out the radius of the base.

PB ES **5** This diagram shows a cylinder with a hemisphere stuck on top.
   The dimensions are as shown.
   Calculate the volume and the surface area of the shape.
   Give your answer in terms of π.

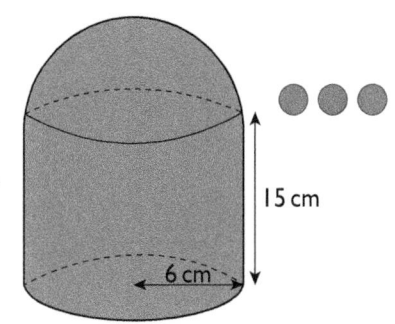

   15 cm
   6 cm

Geometry Strand 6 Three-dimensional shapes Unit 8 Surface area and volume of 3D shapes

DF ES 6 The diagram shows a shape made from a square-based pyramid placed on top of a cube of side 7.5 cm.

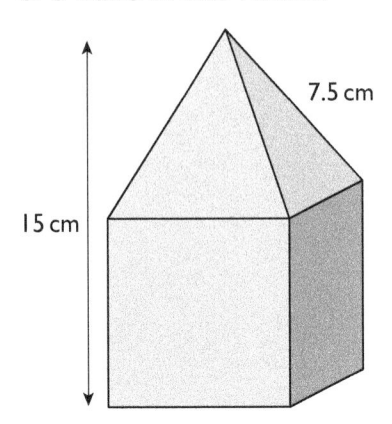

7.5 cm

15 cm

a Work out the volume of the shape.

b Work out the surface area of the shape.

DF ES 7 The diagram shows a cube of side 10 cm with a circular hole of diameter 5 cm drilled through the centre.

Work out

a the volume

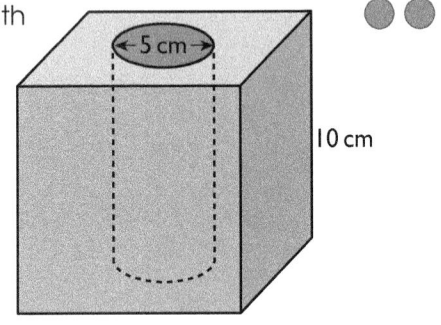

b the surface area.

Give your answers correct to 3 significant figures.

5 cm

10 cm

PB 8 The diagram shows the frustum of a cone. It is made by cutting off the top of a large cone.
The dimensions are as shown.

a Show that the height of the large cone from which the frustum is made is 25 cm.

b Work out the volume of the frustum.

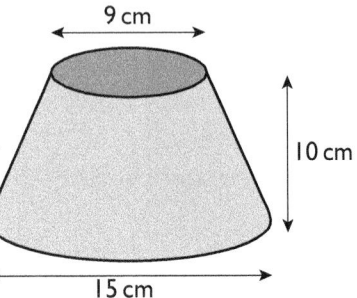

c Work out the curved surface area of the frustum.

Give your answers correct to 3 significant figures.

9 cm

10 cm

15 cm

94

Geometry Strand 6 Three-dimensional shapes Unit 8 Surface area and volume of 3D shapes

9 A sphere of radius r cm has the same volume as a cone with a base radius of $2r$ cm.

  a Prove that the height of the cone h is equal to r.

  b What is the ratio of the surface area of the sphere to the curved surface area of the cone?

10 A company makes steel ball bearings by melting blocks of steel.
The ball bearings are spheres with radius 0.25 cm.
How many ball bearings can be made from a 1 m³ block of steel?
Give your answer to the nearest thousand.

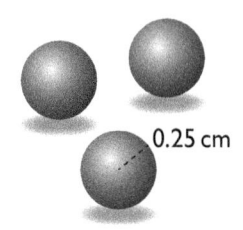

0.25 cm

11 Mr Field wants to buy a new silo to store the cereal crops from his farm.
He has a choice of two cylinders. Both have a cylindrical base of diameter 20 m and height 20 m. Silo A has a hemispherical roof and Silo B has a conical roof.
He wants to buy the silo with the greatest volume.
Which silo will Mr Field buy?
Show your working.

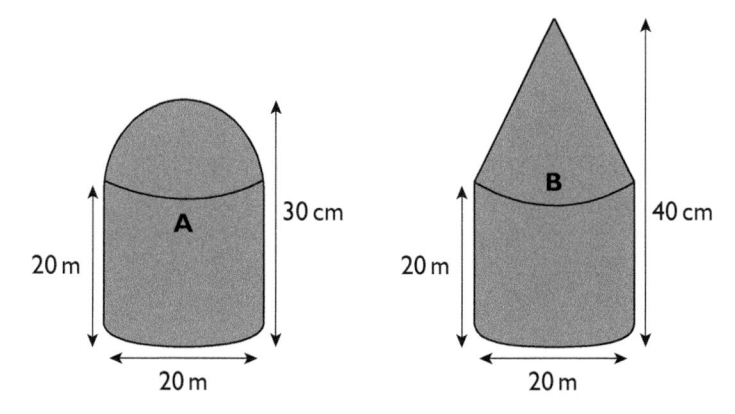

A 30 cm 20 m 20 m

B 40 cm 20 m 20 m

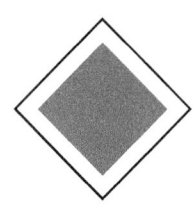

Geometry Strand 7 Vectors
Unit 1 Vectors

PS — PRACTISING SKILLS **DF** — DEVELOPING FLUENCY **PB** — PROBLEM SOLVING **ES** — EXAM-STYLE

PS **1** Work out these vectors.

a $\begin{pmatrix}2\\4\end{pmatrix}+\begin{pmatrix}3\\1\end{pmatrix}$ b $\begin{pmatrix}4\\2\end{pmatrix}-\begin{pmatrix}3\\1\end{pmatrix}$ c $\begin{pmatrix}2\\1\end{pmatrix}-\begin{pmatrix}3\\2\end{pmatrix}$ d $\begin{pmatrix}2\\4\end{pmatrix}-\begin{pmatrix}-3\\-1\end{pmatrix}$

PS **2** Work out these vectors.

a $3\begin{pmatrix}2\\1\end{pmatrix}+2\begin{pmatrix}3\\1\end{pmatrix}$ b $5\begin{pmatrix}2\\4\end{pmatrix}-2\begin{pmatrix}3\\1\end{pmatrix}$ c $2\begin{pmatrix}-2\\3\end{pmatrix}-3\begin{pmatrix}-2\\-3\end{pmatrix}$

DF **3** One of these vectors is not parallel to the others.
ES Which one?

$\begin{pmatrix}4\\3\end{pmatrix}$ $\begin{pmatrix}-4\\-3\end{pmatrix}$ $\begin{pmatrix}5\\4\end{pmatrix}$ $\begin{pmatrix}2\\1.5\end{pmatrix}$ $\begin{pmatrix}8\\6\end{pmatrix}$ $\begin{pmatrix}-2\\-1.5\end{pmatrix}$

PS **4** Write down the vectors **a** to **e** as column vectors.

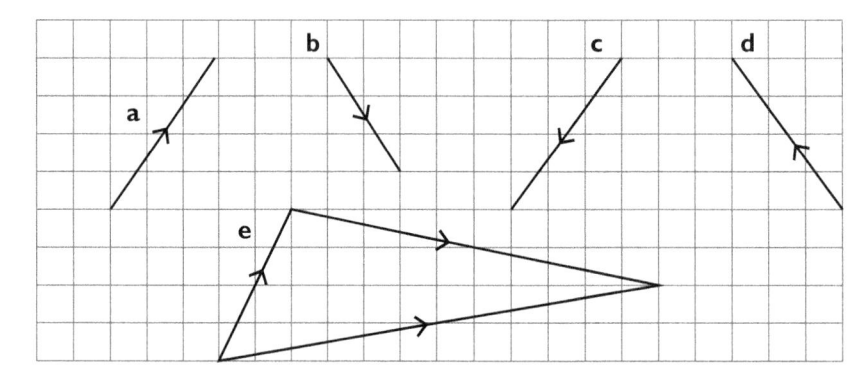

DF **5** $p=\begin{pmatrix}3\\2\end{pmatrix}$ $q=\begin{pmatrix}2\\-1\end{pmatrix}$ $r=\begin{pmatrix}-1\\3\end{pmatrix}$

Show each of these vectors on a square grid.

a 2**p**   b **p** + **q**   c **q** − **r**   d **p** − 3**q**

Geometry Strand 7 Vectors Unit 1 Vectors

6 Work out the value of the letters in these equations.

a $\begin{pmatrix} 2 \\ 4 \end{pmatrix} + \begin{pmatrix} p \\ q \end{pmatrix} = \begin{pmatrix} 6 \\ 2 \end{pmatrix}$
b $3\begin{pmatrix} f \\ 4 \end{pmatrix} + \begin{pmatrix} 4 \\ g \end{pmatrix} = \begin{pmatrix} 7 \\ 2 \end{pmatrix}$
c $2\begin{pmatrix} 2 \\ x \end{pmatrix} - \begin{pmatrix} y \\ 3 \end{pmatrix} = \begin{pmatrix} 6 \\ 5 \end{pmatrix}$

d $5\begin{pmatrix} -2 \\ s \end{pmatrix} - 2\begin{pmatrix} r \\ -3 \end{pmatrix} = \begin{pmatrix} 4 \\ -2 \end{pmatrix}$
e $t\begin{pmatrix} 2 \\ 3 \end{pmatrix} + 2\begin{pmatrix} 3 \\ v \end{pmatrix} = \begin{pmatrix} 4 \\ 2 \end{pmatrix}$
f $2\begin{pmatrix} 3 \\ h \end{pmatrix} - \begin{pmatrix} h \\ j \end{pmatrix} = \begin{pmatrix} 2h \\ 3j \end{pmatrix}$

7 Shape R is reflected in the line $x = -1$ to shape S.

Shape S is reflected in the line $y = 0$ to shape T.

Shape T is rotated 180° about centre (0, −2) to shape U.

What translation maps shape U directly to shape R?

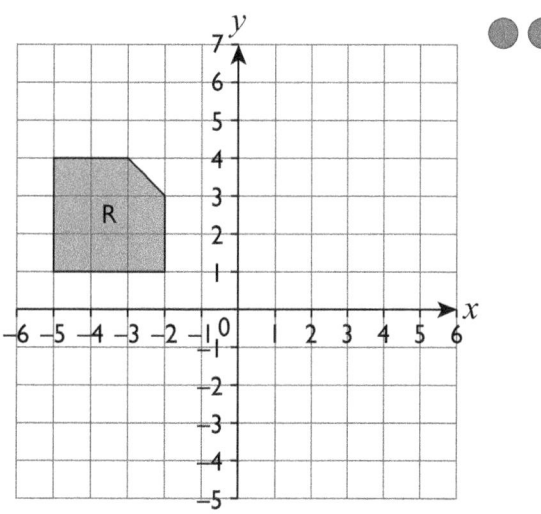

8 $\mathbf{m} = \begin{pmatrix} 3 \\ 2 \end{pmatrix}$ and $\mathbf{n} = \begin{pmatrix} 2 \\ -3 \end{pmatrix}$ are vectors representing two translations.

Deduce the values of p and q for which $p\mathbf{m} + q\mathbf{n}$ is parallel to the vector $\begin{pmatrix} 8 \\ 14 \end{pmatrix}$.

9 The diagram shows O, P and Q.

On this diagram, $\overrightarrow{OP}$ and $\overrightarrow{OQ}$ represent the vectors **p** and **q**.

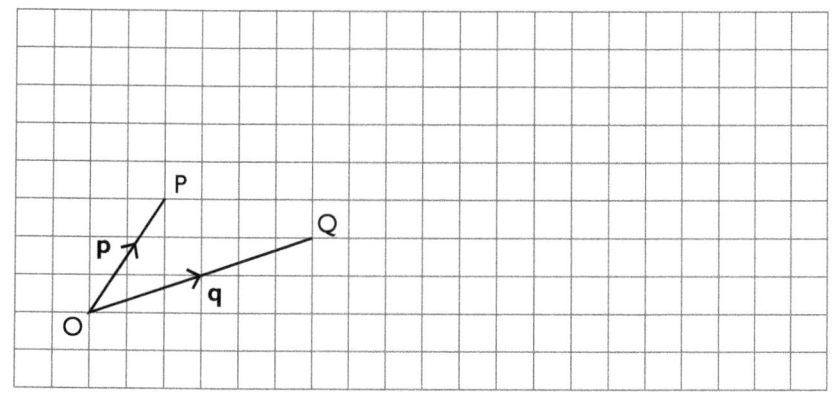

Copy the diagram, then draw these vectors.

a $\overrightarrow{OR}$ where $\mathbf{r} = \mathbf{p} + \mathbf{q}$
b $\overrightarrow{OS}$ where $\mathbf{s} = \mathbf{q} - \mathbf{p}$
c $\overrightarrow{OT}$ where $\mathbf{t} = 2\mathbf{p} + \mathbf{q}$
d $\overrightarrow{OV}$ where $\mathbf{v} = 2\mathbf{q} - \mathbf{p}$

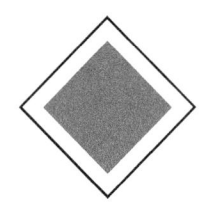

Statistics Strand 2 Draw and interpret statistical diagrams
Unit 5 Displaying grouped data

PS PRACTISING SKILLS **DF** DEVELOPING FLUENCY **PB** PROBLEM SOLVING **ES** EXAM-STYLE

PS 1 State whether each type of data is discrete or continuous. The first one has been done for you.

   a The number of wheels on a bus   *discrete*
   b The time taken to run 100 metres
   c The mass of an elephant
   d The number of bricks in a wall
   e The temperature of a cup of tea
   f The height of a mountain
   g The number of craters on the moon

PS 2 Copy and complete each category so that it has five equal classes.

   a $0 < w \leq 10$ $10 < w \leq 20$ ____   ____   ____
   b $100 \leq t < 150$ ____ $200 \leq t < 250$ ____   ____
   c ____ $15 \leq p < 17.5$ ____ $20 \leq p < 22.5$ ____
   d $125.7 < d \leq 126.2$ $126.2 < d \leq 126.7$ ____   ____   ____
   e ____ $2.5 \leq c < 2.8$ $2.8 \leq c < 3.1$ ____   ____
   f ____   ____ $0.56 < h \leq 0.6$ ____ $0.64 < h \leq 0.68$

PS 3 Neil has recorded the mass of 30 mice. Here are his results, in grams.

12.7	20.7	15.3	22.8	21.3	18.4	15.9	22.1	19.9	13.5
15.1	19.9	24.7	18.9	14.7	22.0	23.4	18.9	22.4	20.4
20.4	17.2	19.5	17.3	19.1	19.7	17.9	21.8	14.1	16.4

a Copy and complete the tally chart.

Mass, m grams	Tally	Frequency
$12.5 < m \leq 15$		
$15 < m \leq 17.5$		
$17.5 < m \leq 20$		
$20 < m \leq 22.5$		
$22.5 < m \leq 25$		

b Write down the modal class.

DF 4 A doctor recorded the body temperatures of a sample of babies. Some of her results are in this frequency diagram.

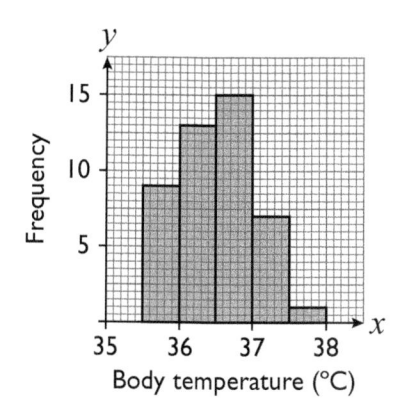

a Copy and complete the table.

Body temperature, x °C	Frequency
$35 < x \leq 35.5$	0
	9
$36 < x \leq 36.5$	
$36.5 < x \leq 37$	
$37.5 < x \leq 38$	1

b How many babies were in the sample?

c Work out the percentage of babies in the sample with a body temperature in the range $36 < x \leq 37$.

Statistics Strand 2 Draw and interpret statistical diagrams Unit 5 Displaying grouped data

5 Monica recorded the time taken, in seconds, to serve individual customers in her shop. Her results are summarised in the frequency table.

Time, t seconds	Frequency
$0 < t \leq 10$	4
$10 < t \leq 20$	8
$20 < t \leq 30$	17
$30 < t \leq 40$	12
$40 < t \leq 50$	9

a It took more than 40 seconds to serve some customers. How many?

b It took 17.5 s to serve Mr Brown. Which group is he in?

c Draw a frequency diagram to show the data.

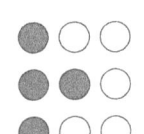

6 The stem-and-leaf diagram gives information about the heights, in metres, of 25 sycamore trees in a wood.

```
0 | 3 5 5 6 6 7 8 9 9 9
1 | 0 2 2 5 4 6 8 9
2 | 2 6 6 7 9
3 | 5 7
```

Key: 3|5 means a tree of height 35 m

a Draw a frequency diagram to show the data.

b Describe the distribution.
What, if anything, does this tell you about the ages of these sycamore trees?

7 Amod recorded the lung capacities of 30 adult males. Here are his results, in litres.

5.6	5.7	5.1	5.9	5.5	5.6	5.1	5.6	6.8	5.3
6.1	5.4	6.2	6.4	5.4	5.7	6.4	6.5	5.9	6.4
5.8	5.9	6.3	5.1	5.8	6.6	5.6	5.3	5.8	6.8

a Make a grouped frequency table for this data, using four equal class intervals.

b Which class contains the median?

c Draw a frequency diagram to show the data.

Statistics Strand 2 Draw and interpret statistical diagrams Unit 5 Displaying grouped data

8 Ori recorded the lengths of time, in seconds, some students could stand on their left leg. His results are in this frequency table.

Time (for left leg) t seconds	Frequency
$50 < t \leq 100$	12
$100 < t \leq 150$	33
$150 < t \leq 200$	20
$200 < t \leq 250$	8
$250 < t \leq 300$	7

He also recorded the lengths of time, in seconds, that these students could stand on their right leg. The results are in this frequency diagram.

Compare the lengths of time that these students could stand on each leg.

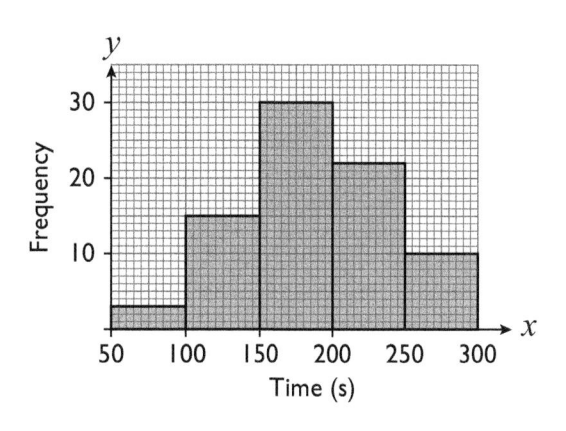

9 William recorded the masses, m kg, of 300 babies. His results are in this pie chart.

   a Use the information in Williams's pie chart to draw a frequency diagram.

   b Cathy says, 'a frequency diagram is a better way to show William's results'. Do you agree with Cathy? Explain why.

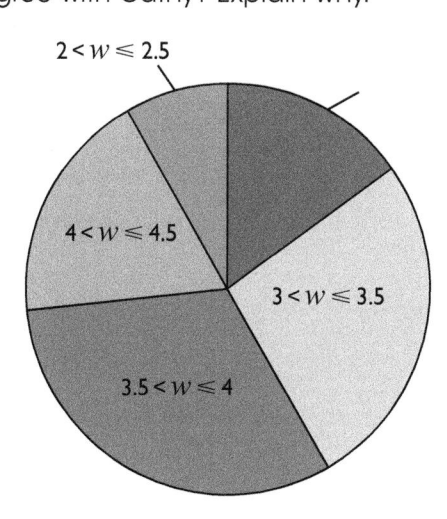

101

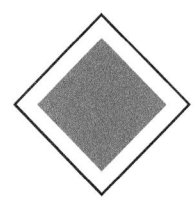

Statistics Strand 2 Draw and interpret statistical diagrams
Unit 6 Scatter diagrams

PS PRACTISING SKILLS   **DF** DEVELOPING FLUENCY   **PB** PROBLEM SOLVING   **ES** EXAM-STYLE

PS 1 a Describe the correlation shown in this scatter diagram.

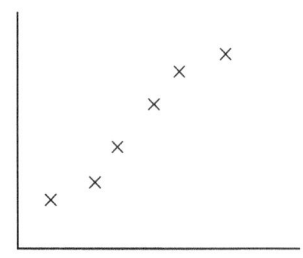

b Draw a scatter diagram to show
  i negative correlation
  ii no correlation.

PS 2 The table shows information about the number of pages and the masses of some paperback books.

ES

Number of pages	80	79	80	96	128	72	120	144	95
Mass (g)	135	125	125	129	164	105	155	171	147

a Draw a scatter diagram for this data.

b Describe the correlation in the scatter diagram.

c Draw a line of best fit.

d The paperback *Overlord* has 100 pages. Use your graph to estimate the mass of this paperback.

e *Superfast* has a mass of 160 g. Use your graph to estimate the number of pages in this paperback.

Statistics Strand 2 Draw and interpret statistical diagrams Unit 6 Scatter diagrams

PS **3** The scatter graph shows the prices and mileages of all the used
ES cars at A1 garage.

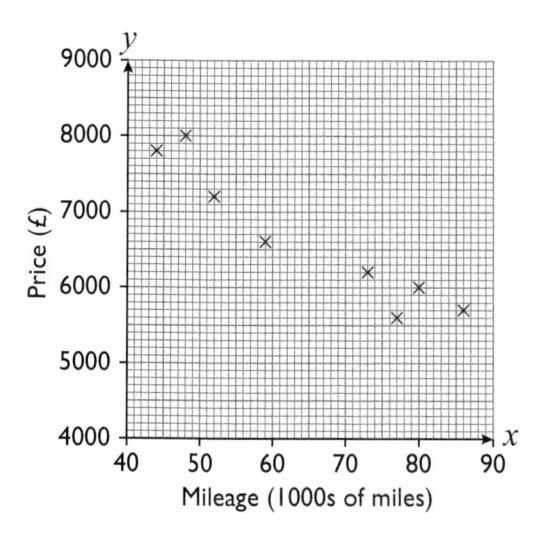

a How many used cars are there at A1 garage?

b What is the mileage of the car with the
   i highest price
   ii lowest price?

c Work out the mean price of all the used cars at A1 garage.

d Describe the correlation in the scatter diagram.

e The garage receives another used car. Its clock shows 65 000 miles. Estimate the selling price of this car.

DF **4** Larry recorded the heights and the foot lengths of the other seven
ES athletes in his squad. His results are shown in this table.

Height (cm)	148	152	154	158	163	168	160
Foot length (cm)	20.5	23	21	24	25	26.5	25

a Draw the scatter diagram.

b Describe the correlation in the scatter diagram.

c Larry's height is 165 cm. Draw a line of best fit and use it to estimate Larry's foot length.

Statistics Strand 2 Draw and interpret statistical diagrams Unit 6 Scatter diagrams

5 A scientist measured the density and the speed of sound in eight different gases. The scatter diagram shows her results.

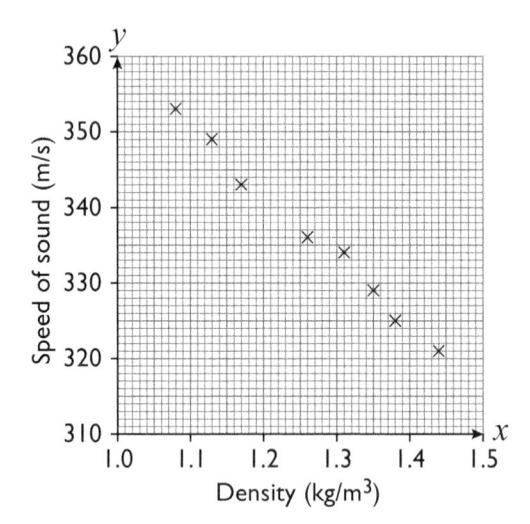

[Scatter diagram: Speed of sound (m/s) on y-axis from 310 to 360, Density (kg/m³) on x-axis from 1.0 to 1.5, showing 8 data points with negative correlation]

  a For one of these gases, the speed of sound is 349 m/s. What is the density of this gas?

  b Describe the correlation shown in the scatter diagram.

  c Draw a line of best fit and use it to predict the speed of sound in a gas that has a density of 1.2 kg/m³.

6 State which type of correlation (positive or negative) is suggested by the following relationships.

  a As the height of an elephant increase, so does its mass.

  b As the age of a tadpole increases, the length of its tail decreases.

  c The greater the amount of fuel in a car's fuel tank, the greater the distance it will travel.

  d The more time people spend working, the less free time they'll have.

  e The greater the height of a weather balloon, the lower the surrounding air temperature.

  f The greater the time spent revising, the greater the number of marks achieved in the test.

7 The table shows information about the body lengths and the wingspans of six British birds.

Bird	A	B	C	D	E	F
Body length (cm)	50–60	25–35	40–45	28–40	60–66	63–65
Wingspan (cm)	100–150	60–65	95–115	60–80	145–165	120–150

104

a Copy and complete the table below for the mid body lengths and mid wingspans for these birds. The first one has been done for you.

Bird	A	B	C	D	E	F
Mid body length (cm)	55					
Mid wingspan (cm)	125					

b Draw the scatter diagram.

c Describe and interpret the correlation between mid body length and mid wingspan.

8 The scatter graph shows information about the number of people visiting an exhibition and the number of brochures sold in the exhibition shop each day last week.

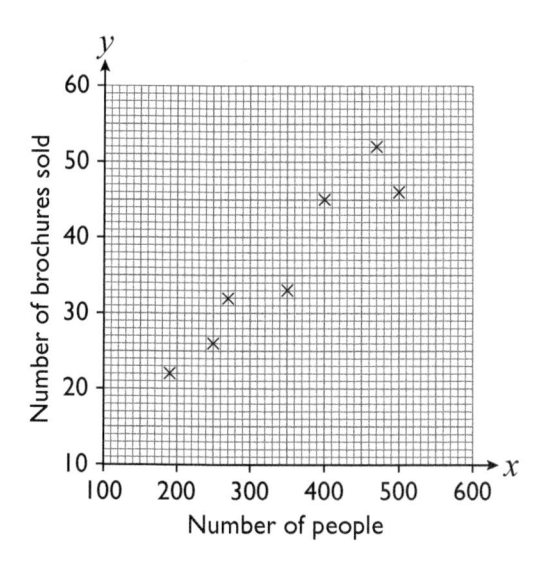

a 45 brochures were sold on Wednesday.
How many people visited the exhibition on Wednesday?

b 250 people visited the exhibition on Monday.
Twice as many people visited the exhibition on Saturday as on Monday.
Work out the difference between the numbers of brochures sold on Saturday and Monday.

c Describe the correlation in the scatter diagram.

d Gary says, 'the day on which the median number of people visited the museum is the same day as the day on which the median number of brochures was sold'.
Is he right? Show how you get your answer.

Statistics Strand 2 Draw and interpret statistical diagrams Unit 6 Scatter diagrams

9 The scatter diagrams show information about the marks given to each of eight cakes, A–H, by three judges in a baking competition.

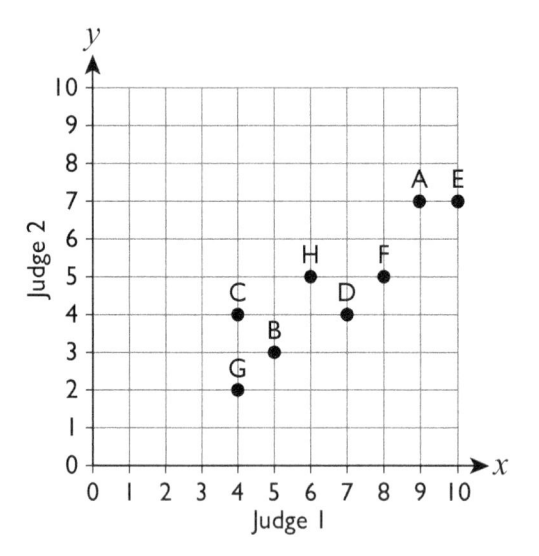

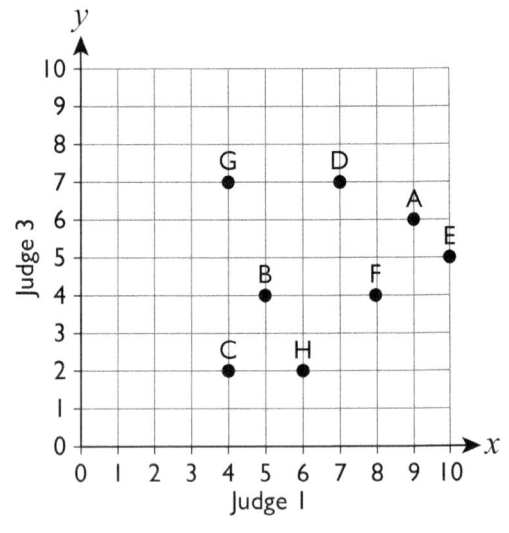

a How consistent are the three judges in their marking? Give reasons for your answer.

b Draw a third scatter diagram to show the marks given to the eight cakes by judges 2 and 3.

c i Describe the correlation in this scatter diagram.
 ii Did you expect this answer? Explain why.

106

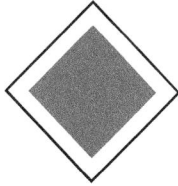

Statistics Strand 2 Draw and interpret statistical diagrams
Unit 7 Using lines of best fit

PS — PRACTISING SKILLS **DF** — DEVELOPING FLUENCY **PB** — PROBLEM SOLVING **ES** — EXAM-STYLE

PS 1 One of the points in this scatter diagram is an outlier.
Copy the scatter diagram and circle the outlier.

PS 2 Choose the most appropriate word from the list below to complete each sentence.

causation negative positive interpolation
extrapolation outlier bivariate trend

a _____ is when you estimate a value beyond the range of the data.

b A scatter diagram is used to show the relationship in _____ data.

c An _____ is a pair of values that does not fit the overall trend.

d Correlation does not prove _____.

e _____ is when you estimate a value within the range of the data.

DF / ES 3 The table shows the heights and masses of ten players in a football team.

Player	1	2	3	4	5	6	7	8	9	10
Height (cm)	177	138	184	182	180	178	176	172	170	169
Mass (kg)	114	121	119	117	116	116	115	111	108	110

a Which player is the shortest?

b Draw a scatter diagram for this data.

c Draw a line of best fit.

d Helmut is also in this football team. His height is 175 cm. Use your line of best fit to estimate the difference between Helmut's mass and the mass of the heaviest player.

107

Statistics Strand 2 Draw and interpret statistical diagrams Unit 7 Using lines of best fit

PS 4 This scatter diagram shows the distances and costs of nine train journeys.

A line of best fit has been drawn on the scatter diagram.

a Giles travels on a train journey that costs him £17.05. Use the line of best fit to estimate the distance he travelled.

b Sophie is going to travel 58 km by train. Use the line of best fit to estimate the cost of Sophie's journey.

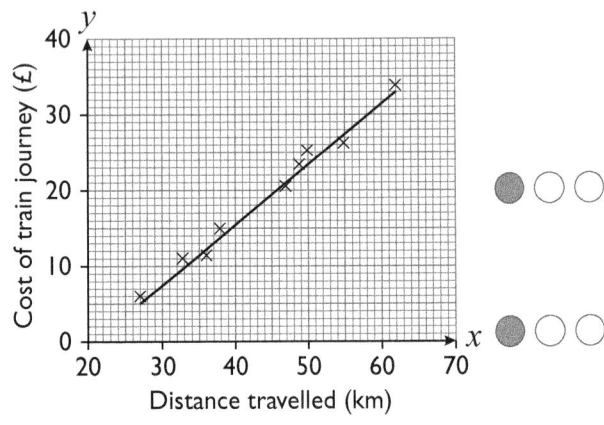

c Jim is going to travel 70 km by train. Use the line of best fit to estimate the cost of Jim's journey.

DF ES 5 The scatter diagram shows the number of traffic cameras and the number of speeding fines per year in a particular region of the UK over a nine-year period.

A line of best fit has been drawn on the scatter diagram.

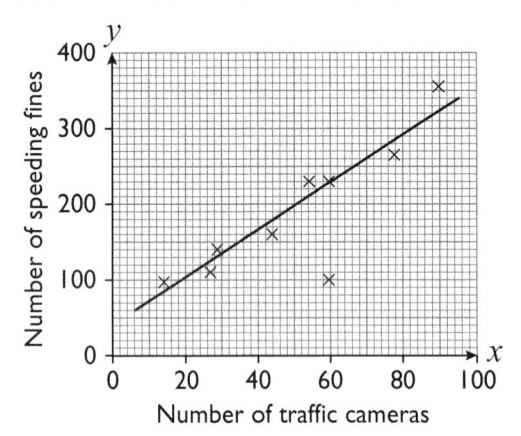

a Identify any possible outliers in the data.

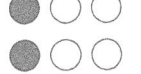

b Describe and interpret the correlation in the scatter diagram.

c Pete says that traffic cameras cause people to speed. Is he right? Give reasons for your answer.

Statistics Strand 2 Draw and interpret statistical diagrams Unit 7 Using lines of best fit

6 Ulrich measured the wind speed and the air temperature at 1 pm on each of 7 days.
Here are his results.

Wind speed (x km/h)	15.6	8.9	22.1	9.4	0.5	5.8	18.7
Air temperature (y °C)	17.5	20.3	17.8	23.2	19.7	17.5	19.2

  a Draw a scatter diagram of Ulrich's measurements.

  b Is there any correlation between wind speed and air temperature? Give a reason for your answer.

  c A weather forecaster says that the wind speed at 1 pm tomorrow will be 25 km/h.

  Ulrich says he is going to draw a line of best fit on the scatter diagram and use it to estimate the air temperature for a wind speed of 25 km/h.

  Comment on the reliability of Ulrich's estimate.

7 Charlie is investigating how long it takes paint to dry. He conducts eight experiments in which he paints a wall and records the time it takes for the paint to dry and the average air temperature during this period. Here are his results.

Experiment	Time	Temperature
1	12 hours	3.6 °C
2	6 hours	6.8 °C
3	5 hours 15 minutes	12.9 °C
4	4 hours 30 minutes	18.4 °C
5	4 hours	24.1 °C
6	3 hours 30 minutes	28.7 °C
7	3 hours 15 minutes	32.2 °C
8	2 hours 45 minutes	35.3 °C

  a Draw a scatter diagram of Charlie's results.

  b Identify the outlier.

  c Charlie thinks that there is a relationship between the time it takes for the paint to dry and the average air temperature. Is he right? Explain your answer.

Statistics Strand 2 Draw and interpret statistical diagrams Unit 7 Using lines of best fit

8 The scatter diagram shows information about the time taken for each of eight students to write the same text message first with their left hand and then with their right hand.

a Mary is one of these students. It took her 17.5s to write the text message with her right hand. How long did Mary take to write the text message with her left hand?

b Work out the mean time taken for these students to write the text message with their
  i left hand
  ii right hand.

c Compare the means.

d One of these students may be left handed. Which student? Give a reason for your answer.

e Describe the correlation in the scatter diagram.

9 Lorna recorded the resistance of an electronic component at eight different temperatures. The table shows her results.

Temperature (°C)	10	15	20	25	30	35	40	45
Resistance (Ω (Ohms))	3575	3300	2925	2550	2125	1825	1400	1350

a Draw a scatter diagram to show the data.

b Calculate
  i the mean temperature ($\bar{x}$)
  ii the mean resistance ($\bar{y}$).

c Plot the point ($\bar{x}, \bar{y}$) on your scatter diagram.

d Draw a line of best fit on your scatter diagram so that it passes through the point ($\bar{x}, \bar{y}$).

e Use your line of best fit to estimate the resistance of the component at
  i 22.5°C
  ii 50°C.

f Which of these two estimates is likely to be more accurate? Explain why.

110

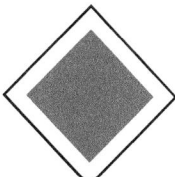

Statistics Strand 4 Probability
Unit 4 Estimating probability

PS — PRACTISING SKILLS **DF** — DEVELOPING FLUENCY **PB** — PROBLEM SOLVING **ES** — EXAM-STYLE

PS 1 Ben rolls a biased dice 350 times. He rolls 75 sixes. Estimate the probability that Ben rolls a six on his next roll.

PS 2 Bobby throws darts at a dartboard. He is trying to hit the centre of the board. Each time he throws a dart, he records whether he hits the centre (H) or misses the centre (M). Here are his results.

M M M M H M M M M M
M H M H H M M M M M
M M M M M M M M M M
H M H M H

Estimate the probability that Bobby hits the centre of the dartboard with his next throw.

PS 3 Write down the statistical meaning of each of these terms.

  a population   **b** sample   **c** random sample   **d** trial

DF 4 On her way to work, Heidi passes one set of traffic lights. Over a 30-day period, she had to stop at the lights 16 times.

Heidi thinks she is unlucky with the traffic lights. She says, 'when I drive to work tomorrow, the probability that I will have to stop at the traffic lights is greater than 0.5'.

Is Heidi right? Give a reason for your answer.

DF 5 The table shows the number of games won, lost and drawn for two teams in a handball league.

Team	Games won	Games lost	Games drawn
Stylish Snatchers	12	7	5
Golden Grabbers	18	12	10

  a Which team has played more games?

  b The Stylish Snatchers and the Golden Grabbers are going to play each other in their next game. From the information in the table, which of these two teams is more likely to win the game? Give a reason for your answer.

Statistics Strand 4 Probability Unit 4 Estimating probability

6 Zoe wants to find the probability that a spider selected at random is female. She looks at five samples of spiders and records the gender of each spider. The table shows her results.

Sample	1	2	3	4	5
Sample size	10	25	50	90	1250
Number of females	8	19	38	68	937
Relative frequency	0.8				

a Copy and complete the table.

b Which of these relative frequencies gives the best estimate for the probability that a spider selected at random will be female? Give a reason for your answer.

c Use the information in the table to find a better estimate for this probability.

7 Pam owns a coffee shop. She offers a free biscuit with each hot drink she sells.

Each customer having a hot drink can choose from a digestive biscuit, a custard cream or a bourbon biscuit.

The two-way table shows some information about the biscuits chosen by 150 customers.

	Digestive biscuit	Custard cream	Bourbon biscuit	Total
Male	25			78
Female		32		
Total	37	48		

a Copy and complete the two-way table.

b Estimate the probability that the next customer that buys a hot drink at the coffee shop will

   i choose a custard cream

   ii be male and choose a digestive.

c Pam says that males are more likely to choose a bourbon biscuit than females.

Is she right? Show how you get your answer.

8 The table shows the types and numbers of tyres sold by a tyre shop last week.

Type of tyre	AB303	AC415	XX137	TK700
Number of tyres	36	27	45	58

A customer wants to buy a tyre at the shop.

a Estimate the probability that this customer will buy a TK700 tyre.

b The stock of tyres in the shop is getting low. The manager is going to order a total of 1000 tyres to replace the stock.
How many of each type of tyre should she order?

9 Last week, 109 people donated blood at a clinic. The bar chart shows information about the number of donors and their blood groups (O, A, B and AB).

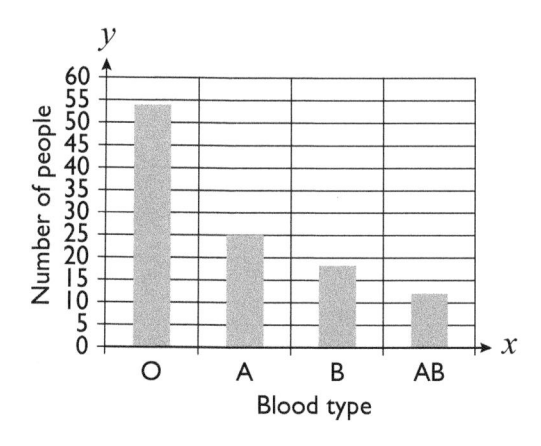

a Estimate the probability that the next person to donate blood at the clinic will have blood type A.

b There are a total of 980 people registered to donate blood at the clinic.

The table shows information about the number of donations made by these registered donors during the last year.

Number of donations	0	1	2	3
Number of people	175	525	170	80

i Show that the total number of donations during the last year was 1105.

ii Estimate the number of donations of blood type O during the last year. Explain why this is an estimate.

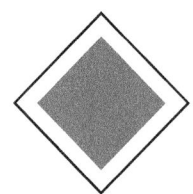

Statistics Strand 4 Probability
Unit 5 The multiplication rule

PS PRACTISING SKILLS   **DF** DEVELOPING FLUENCY   **PB** PROBLEM SOLVING   **ES** EXAM-STYLE

PS **1** A box contains three blue pens and six black pens.

  a Celine takes a pen at random from the box. Write down the probability that the pen will be
   i blue
   ii black.

  b She puts the first pen back and takes a blue pen from the box.
   How many
   i blue pens
   ii black pens
   are now in the box?

  c Celine does not replace the blue pen and takes another pen from the box at random. Write down the probability that the pen is
   i blue
   ii black.

PS **2** Bag A contains 3 red counters and 2 blue counters.
   Bag B contains 2 red counters and 5 blue counters.

  a Copy and complete this tree diagram.

   Kerry takes 1 counter from bag A and 1 counter from bag B without looking.

  b Work out the probability that both counters will be
   i red
   ii blue.

  c Work out the probability that the counter from bag A will be blue and the counter from bag B will be red.

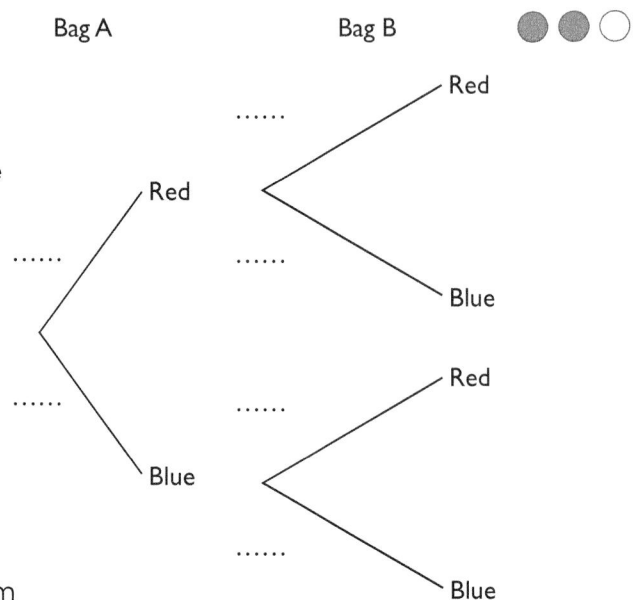

Statistics Strand 4 Probability Unit 5 The multiplication rule

PS 3 William has a fair five-sided spinner like the one in the diagram.
He is going to spin the spinner twice.
Work out the probability the spinner lands on

  a A followed by A

  b A followed by B

  c B followed by C.

William now spins the spinner three times. work out the probability the spinner lands on

  d A followed by A followed by C.

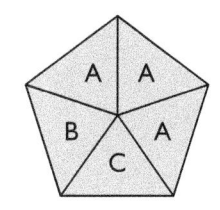

PS 4 A box contains 7 lemon sweets and 6 lime sweets.
Mary takes 2 sweets from the box at random.
Copy and complete the tree diagram.

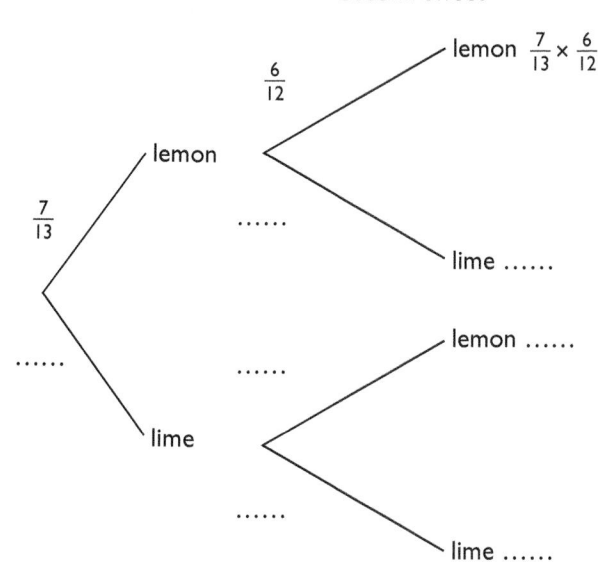

First sweet   Second sweet

lemon $\frac{7}{13} \times \frac{6}{12}$

$\frac{6}{12}$

lemon

$\frac{7}{13}$

lime ......

......

lemon ......

......

lime

......

lime ......

DF 5 Polly has a bag of coins and a box of coins.
Without looking, she takes a coin from the bag and a coin from the box.

The probability that the coin from the bag is a £1 coin is $\frac{4}{7}$.

The probability that the coin from the box is a £1 coin is $\frac{3}{4}$.

  a Work out the probability that the coin from the bag and the coin from the box are both £1 coins.

  b Work out the probability that the coin from the bag is a £1 coin and the coin from the box is not a £1 coin.

  c Write down the situation represented by the calculation $\frac{3}{7} \times \frac{1}{4} = \frac{3}{28}$.

6 Tom and Simone both think of a number from 1 to 9 inclusive.

  a Work out the probability that they both think of
   i 3
   ii an even number
   iii a number greater or equal to 7
   iv a prime number.

  b Work out the probability that
   i Tom thinks of a number greater than 3 and Simone thinks of a number less than 5
   ii Tom thinks of a square number and Simone thinks of a prime number.

7 Zoe takes two tests, A and B.

The probability that she passes test A is 35% and the probability that she passes test B is 85%.

The events are independent.

Work out the probability that Zoe will

  a pass both the tests
  b fail both tests
  c pass only one of the tests.

8 Vicky and Mica are playing a game. They each need to roll a six on a normal six-sided die to start the game.

  a What is the probability that Vicky will start the game on her
   i first roll
   ii second roll?

  b What is the probability that Mica will start the game on his fifth roll of the dice?

9 Sri wears a shirt and a tie to work.

The probability that Sri wears a white shirt is 0.8.

When Sri wears a white shirt, the probability that he wears a pink tie is 0.75.

When Sri does not wear a white shirt, the probability that he wears a pink tie is 0.35.

  a Draw a tree diagram to represent this situation. Fill in all the probabilities.

  b Work out the probability that Sri does not wear a pink tie when he goes to work tomorrow.

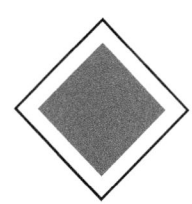

Statistics Strand 4 Probability
Unit 6 The addition rule

PS – PRACTISING SKILLS   **DF** – DEVELOPING FLUENCY   **PB** – PROBLEM SOLVING   **ES** – EXAM-STYLE

PS 1 The Venn diagram shows information about a box that contains red beads, blue beads and yellow beads.

   a How many beads are there in the box?

  A bead is taken at random from the box.

   b Write down the probability that it is
     i red
     ii yellow.

   c Write down the probability that it is
     i red or blue
     ii blue or yellow.

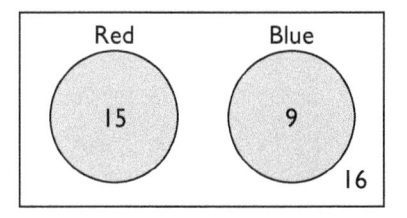

(Venn diagram: Red circle contains 15, Blue circle contains 9, outside 16)

PS 2 The Venn diagram shows information about the numbers of students studying Chinese, Japanese and other languages in a college.
One of these students is chosen at random.

   a Work out the probability that this student studies
     i Chinese and Japanese
     ii Chinese or Japanese
     iii only Japanese.

   b Work out the probability that this student does not study
     i Japanese
     ii Chinese.

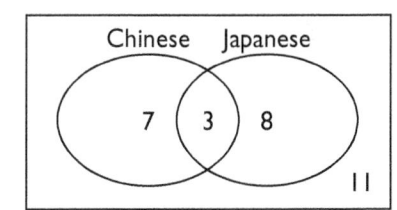

(Venn diagram: Chinese only 7, intersection 3, Japanese only 8, outside 11)

PS 3 a Event A and event B are mutually exclusive events.
P(A) = 0.48 and P(B) = 0.37.
    i Draw a Venn diagram showing this information.
    ii Find P(A or B).

   b Event C and event D are not mutually exclusive events.
P(C) = 0.8, P(D) = 0.5 and P(C and D) = 0.4.
    i Draw a Venn diagram showing this information.
    ii Find P(C or D).

Statistics Strand 4 Probability Unit 6 The addition rule

4 65% of the people at a party arrived by taxi and 80% arrived in fancy dress.

55% arrived by taxi and in fancy dress.

   a Draw a Venn diagram to show this information.

   b Work out the probability that a person chosen at random arrived by taxi or wore fancy dress.

5 Giles asks 52 people which, if any, of three coffee shops they go to. Here are his results.

- 15 people go to coffee shop A.
- 25 people go to coffee shop B.
- 12 people go to coffee shop C.
- 8 people go to coffee shop A and coffee shop B.
- 10 people do not go to any of these coffee shops.

   a Copy and complete the Venn diagram to show this information.

   b Work out the probability that a person chosen at random
   - **i** goes only to coffee shop A
   - **ii** does not go to coffee shop B
   - **iii** goes to coffee shop A or coffee shop B
   - **iv** goes to coffee shop A or coffee shop C.

   c Given that a person goes to coffee shop A or coffee shop B, what is the probability that they also go to coffee shop C?

6 There are 120 computers in a showroom.

86 have a 5 GB video card.

75 have a RAM extension pack.

Giles picks one of the computers at random.

What is the probability that he picks a computer with both a 5 GB video card and a RAM extension pack?

7 Judy asks 100 people which, if any, of her three favourite films they have watched.

Here is some information about her results.

- 49 have watched Casablanca.
- 47 have watched The Big Sleep.
- 51 have watched The Maltese Falcon.
- 25 have watched Casablanca and The Maltese Falcon.
- 23 have watched Casablanca and The Big Sleep.
- 24 have watched The Big Sleep and The Maltese Falcon.
- 10 have watched all three films.

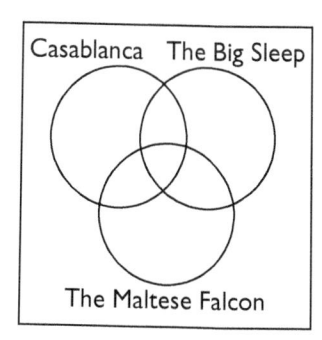

[Venn diagram with three overlapping circles labelled Casablanca, The Big Sleep, and The Maltese Falcon]

a Copy and complete the Venn diagram.

b Write down the probability that a person chosen at random has not watched any of these films.

c Work out the probability that a person chosen at random has watched
  i The Big Sleep
  ii Casablanca or The Big Sleep
  iii The Big Sleep or The Maltese Falcon
  iv Casablanca or The Maltese Falcon or The Big Sleep.

8 A box contains orange sweets, strawberry sweets, lime sweets and lemon sweets.
The probability of selecting an orange sweet at random is 0.18.
The probability of selecting a strawberry sweet at random is 0.25.
The probability of selecting a lime sweet at random is 0.37.
Work out the probability of selecting, at random

a an orange sweet or a strawberry sweet

b a strawberry sweet or a lemon sweet.

9 Bob is going to play a game of tennis and a game of chess.
The probability that he wins at tennis is $\frac{3}{7}$.

The probability that he wins at chess is $\frac{2}{5}$.
The events are independent.
Work out the probability that Bob will win at tennis or chess.

10 $P(A) = 0.3$ $P(B) = 0.8$ $P(A \text{ or } B) = 0.86$
Show that event A and event B are independent events.

Owend by:

Sanuja - M
10JD
Taipon School